EUREKA SPRINGS

CITY *of* HEALING WATERS

JUNE WESTPHAL & KATE COOPER

Charleston · London

THE
History
PRESS

Published by The History Press
Charleston, SC 29403
www.historypress.net

Cover art by Jody Stephenson

Front Cover: Painting *Grotto Vigil* by Eureka Springs artist Jody Stephenson, Studio 62.
Back Cover: "Crescent Spring Falls" by Christopher H. Fischer.

Unless otherwise credited, photographs are courtesy of the Eureka Springs, Arkansas
Historic Photo Collection, which includes materials from Eureka Springs Historical
Museum, Carnegie Public Library, Cornerstone Bank (formerly Bank of Eureka Springs)
and nearly forty other collections, digitized by Glenna Booth in 2009.

First published 2012
Manufactured in the United States

ISBN 978.1.60949.650.0

Westphal, June.
Eureka Springs : city of healing waters / June Westphal and Kate Cooper.
p. cm.
Includes bibliographical references.
ISBN 978-1-60949-650-0
1. Eureka Springs (Ark.)--History. I. Cooper, Kate, 1962- II. Title.

F419.E8W47 2012
976.7'17--dc23
2012006919

Notice: The information in this book is true and complete to the best of our knowledge. It is
offered without guarantee on the part of the authors or The History Press. The authors and
The History Press disclaim all liability in connection with the use of this book.

CONTENTS

ACKNOWLEDGEMENTS

This book is dedicated to all people whose lives have been touched by our springs. It is the result of a long process of gathering sources from individuals and collections. In 2003, at a meeting held at the Eureka Springs Historical Museum, a small group of volunteers interested in doing a project on Springs history consulted with June Westphal. She advised them that many sources were available, but they were scattered among many libraries and collections. Thus began a number of projects to locate and scan everything we could find. We would like to thank Jama Best and the Arkansas Humanities Council for their support, as well as Ginni Miller, with the Eureka Springs Historical Museum, who ran to the third floor many times to find materials for us.

Members of the Springs Committee of the Parks and Recreation Commission have provided expertise, encouragement, inspiration and a laptop computer for organizing and analyzing the mountain of data and for writing this manuscript. To the many people in the community who have provided moral support for this work, we thank you. We would also like to thank our families for their sacrifices during the process and for their pride in us. The eyes of the heart shine through you all.

Introduction
CITY OF HEALING WATERS

The sound of water trickling from a rock ledge, a shady nook, wild flowers delicate and fragrant, rest and relaxation were sought and found by many a weary health seeker. Thirst quenched, vitality improving, they walked up and over the hills and explored the hollows. Many moved on or went home often noticeably restored to wellness, and many stayed. Eureka Springs in northwest Arkansas was founded on the belief that healing could be gained from the pure waters that poured out abundantly from deep in the ground.

The history presented in this book is the story of people intimately tied to their environment. The landscape itself becomes like a character, ancient and demanding, giving, renewing, pleasing and at times frustrating.

In chapter one, we provide a brief look into the ancient rock layers through which our springs flow and a scientific glimpse into the great forces that raised the Ozarks.

People have been walking these hills for more than ten thousand years, and while we don't know exactly how they used the springs, we know of some of their ways of adapting and innovating. In chapter two, we combine archaeology and oral history to give the reader an idea of the great changes ancient tribal peoples endured and what they learned.

Chapter three examines historic Indians and the first Europeans who encountered them.

Colonial, territorial and even early statehood are periods in which political boundaries were being drawn, often from great distances away. On the ground, people cared deeply about finding good water and knew how to describe the terrain based on its water resources. Finding a good match between the healthiness of a locale and one's own constitution was important for those who came west. Chapters four and five tell the stories of hunters and pioneers in the area long before the settlement of Eureka Springs.

Crescent Spring Falls. *Photo by Christopher H. Fischer.*

During the American post–Civil War period, people had few options when dealing with illnesses. The healing of a prominent judge was the catalyst needed to begin a mass migration. It was a gathering of weary souls, many coming in search of miracles and many looking on in amazement. As word spread of seemingly miraculous healings, more and more people arrived. Within three years, the population went from a handful to twenty thousand.

Chapters six and seven cover the first rush to the springs and the early settlement period. Chapters eight, nine and ten chart the transition from encampment to a health spa city.

Medicine began to improve, and Eureka Springs moved along with the flow. Chapters eleven through fourteen highlight the dramatic changes brought about during the early to mid-twentieth century. Chapters fifteen, sixteen and seventeen cover the modern era from the centennial to the twenty-first century. Preservation and renovation went alongside the emerging environmental movement, and not always very harmoniously. The centennial, 1979, brought a renewed interest in the historic beginnings of the town. Restoration of many structures, gardening in spring reservations and an extensive exfiltration study were all inspired by the springs and their legacy.

Finally, "Recharge!" concludes the book with answers to a few frequently asked questions and our conclusions and ponderings about the future.

Eureka Springs today is a tourist center. The eclectic shopping district, relaxing spa treatments and luxury Victorian bed-and-breakfast inns are modern reminders of the early heritage. Listed on the National Register of Historic Places since 1970, the historic district attracts nearly one million visitors a year who come to see this well-preserved and unique late nineteenth-century spa, as well as to enjoy the scenic beauty and natural environment surrounding it.

Chapter 1

NATURAL HISTORY

E ureka historian Professor L.J. Kalklosch mentioned a hillside northeast of town that early residents called the "Petrified Forest," where fossils of shells, nuts, acorns and various kinds of wood were found in 1881. In some places like this one, almost any rock a person picks up contains some evidence of seashells or other fossils formed long ago.

ROCK LAYERS OF EUREKA SPRINGS

Ancient volcanic rocks have been found below the surface in Arkansas, indicating that molten rock covered the region during the Precambrian era. The fossil record found in the sedimentary rock in the hills of Eureka Springs contains evidence of life that existed during what geologists call the Paleozoic era. Paleozoic means "ancient life." The several hundred million years of the Paleozoic era are punctuated by major growth spurts and evolutionary leaps, beginning with the greatest burst of evolution in the history of life called the Cambrian explosion.[1]

Major shifts occurred during the Ordovician period between 520 and 440 million years ago. A wide variety of marine invertebrates lived in the oceans, while lichens and mosses began to colonize the land. In the warm, shallow water that covered the site that is now the Ozarks, new types of ecosystems evolved. Coral reefs teemed with trilobites, snails and early versions of clams, oysters, octopus and squid. Scallop-like brachiopods hopped along the bottom. Crinods, relatives of sea urchins and starfish, appeared later in the period.

These layers, the Ordovician Cotter and Powell formations, can be walked on today in the deepest valleys of downtown Eureka Springs.[2] Since

Left: Sycamore Spring.

Below: Fossil showing two sides of one trilobite, six inches in length. *Eureka Springs Historical Museum Collection.*

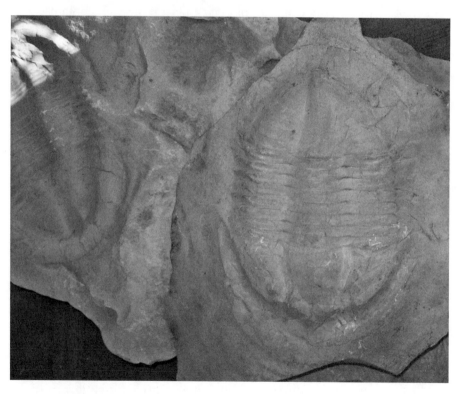

Layers of Ordovician Cotter and Powell formations exposed in road cut on Route 187 south of Beaver Dam. The weathered soil slope above the Sylamore sandstone ledge is the Chattanooga shale. St. Joe limestone is under the grassy slope. *Photo by Jim Helwig.*

sediment deposited later was laid on top of the older layers, moving up the hillside is like coming forward in time in the fossil record.

Between the Ordovician and Silurian periods, a mass extinction occurred. Cooling of the global climate caused a glacier to cover much of South America, Africa, Antarctica and Australia, which were joined together as one huge continent. The Appalachians began to form as land masses collided.[3]

The Sylamore sandstone layer formed during the Silurian period. Aquatic arthropods moved to land. Trilobites decreased in population, while insects, spiders, crabs and centipedes crawled out of the sea and onto the beaches and water scorpions grew to sizes of five to ten feet in length. Sand deposited on the ancient sea floor at that time would become sandstone.

During the next period, the Devonian, land plants developed the vascular systems needed to carry water and food between the roots and leaves. They also developed seeds, which allowed them to spread farther from shore. Following the insects, a four-footed vertebrate developed the ability to live out of water. Most life was still in the oceans, and the Devonian period is known as the "Age of Fish." A mass extinction at the end of the Devonian period affected species in water habitats such as sponges and corals more than species living on land.

A shallow sea covered much of the interior of the continent. North America and Europe had merged into what some have called the Old Red Sandstone Continent. Other names for it are Laurussia and Euramerica. It was near the equator in a place with great calm and few winds known as doldrums. Because of this, sediments deposited during this period have properties that make the rocks a key layer in the groundwater system. The lack of winds created stagnant conditions that lasted twenty million years.

Uranium-scavenging bacteria accumulated uranium from sea water and fell to the bottom, where stagnant conditions kept the uranium from reacting. Salts and uranium built up in the layer that came to be called the Chattanooga shale layer.[4] Chattanooga shale extends from the Appalachians across much of the United States, as well as into Canada and Mexico. It is a confining unit in aquifers. Because it is nonporous, water cannot seep through it easily. Spring Street, as well as Douglas and Steele Streets, were built on this layer, which was a natural flat spot and also where many prominent historic springs were located.

The layers that form the highest elevations of the hills of Eureka Springs are called St. Joe limestone and Boone limestone. These were deposited in the

Looking south from Harding Spring bluff, a natural rock shelf formed a relatively flat ledge midway up the hillside on which Spring Street was built.

Mississippian epoch between 360 and 320 million years ago. The shallow sea that covered the Ozarks was home to many animals that contributed their shells to form limestone. Lush evergreens and ferns grew on land. High humidity and oxygen levels allowed insects to diversify and grow large. For example, an ancestor of the dragonfly had a two-foot wingspan. This also aided amphibians as they made the transition to live the adult portion of their lives on land.

Raising the Ozarks

The movements of the continents have had major impacts on the environment and on life as it evolved on Earth. Tracking shifts in the Earth's crust by satellite and Global Positioning System (GPS) technologies, scientists have confirmed that tectonic plates move at rates of two to fifteen centimeters per year.

All the land masses moved together at the end of the Paleozoic era, creating one supercontinent called Pangaea. The Ozarks were near the middle of the C-shaped continent that stretched from the south pole to the north pole. The interior of the huge landmass was dry. Swampland dried up, and plants that could adapt to dryer conditions survived. The ginkgo is one seed plant that survived from this period.

A series of as many as six uplifts raised the Ozark, Boston and Ouachita Mountains above sea level and formed a depression that became the Arkansas River Valley. The uplifted seabed of the early Ozark Dome was deeply fractured. Where stratified sedimentary rock was exposed, cracks widened into rough, jagged valleys.

Massive climate changes and loss of shallow ocean habitat resulted in the most severe mass extinction in Earth's history. Approximately 95 percent of all marine species and nearly as many terrestrial species disappeared during the mass extinction that ended the Paleozoic era about 250 million years ago.

The era following the Paleozoic is called the Mesozoic era. Its three periods—the Triassic, Jurassic and Cretaceous—are the 140 million years when dinosaurs roamed the land. Survivors of the Permian extinction adapted to fill all the available niches. Birds were new. Seed plants, especially conifers, thrived in the north, while seed ferns gravitated to the south. The first flowering plants developed. The first mammals were small, much like lizards with hair, scampering in the shadows of the big reptiles.

There are many ancient species that are endemic to the White River Basin, meaning they live here and nowhere else. The William's crayfish, long-pincered crayfish, yoke darter and checkered madtom are among these.[5]

Chapter 2

PREHISTORIC PEOPLES

PALEO-INDIANS

Paleo-Indians, the first people in the Americas, were ice age hunters who most likely followed woolly mammoths across a land bridge. Native American storytelling traditions have passed down glimpses of what life may have been like for those who migrated to an unknown new world.

Paula Underwood translated and wrote down an Iroquois oral history of an ocean-side people forced to leave their home after a devastating tsunami. The small tribe consisting of thirty-five adults who could carry packs and seventeen others who were children or those who needed assistance made a dangerous, icy crossing from Asia along a path called "Walk by Waters." After many generations, their descendants crossed the plains from the Rocky Mountains into the central Mississippi Valley.

The ancient Hopi clans were guided by special stars as they journeyed in search of their ultimate home in the Southwest, and a magical jar was planted to make a spring appear if fresh water could not be found.[6] The Osage ancestors wandered across the land, marching in a specific order: first the Water People, followed by the Land People and after them the Sky People.[7]

Modern marine archaeology may reveal further sites along ancient coastlines, as well as possible water routes to the Americas. Archaeologists call the people of the transition time between Paleo-Indian and Archaic who lived in Missouri, Arkansas and Oklahoma the Dalton people. The spear points used by the Dalton people were smaller than the previously used Clovis points, showing their adaptation to a wider range of game. Multiuse points were also utilized for domestic purposes. They were hunter-foragers as before but show more evidence of ceremonialism. Iron pigments, possibly used for ceremony, may indicate the beginning of the tradition of body painting. Their camps may have included separate base camps, hunting or task camps and cemeteries.[8] The Slone site on the Cache River may be the oldest cemetery in the Western Hemisphere.[9]

ARCHAIC COMMUNITIES

The Archaic period followed the Paleo-Indian period. During the first two thousand years of the Archaic era, life was extremely stressful for the people of North America. The tundra and forests of the Northeast, including what is now northern Arkansas, turned to "hot wastelands barely fit for humans or animals."[10]

Early Archaic people had to learn to change their diet from what their ancestors had eaten for thirty thousand years during the ice age. Changing from eating almost entirely animal food to around 60 percent plant food probably happened by trial and error over many generations.

Unlike the fat-storing megafauna of the ice age, deer were lean. Although it was a favorite of the ancestors of the Caddo people, hunters who tried to live on venison alone would suffer terrible fatigue and die of "fat starvation." Nuts and oily vegetables provided the required nutrients.

Originally used as a container, the Ozark wild gourd is very likely the wild ancestor of today's acorn and crookneck squashes. It has a history separate from pumpkins, which were domesticated in Mexico. On the edge of the prairie plains and the woodlands, somewhat protected from the great sea of stampeding bison (Dark Ocean), people began to select seeds from the best oily and starchy food plants, such as squash, goosefoot and sunflower. According to Paula Underwood:

> *They saw how it was*
> *that the same trees*
> *that discouraged a Dark Ocean*
> *also discouraged any encouraged seed,*
> *so it became a great preoccupation*
> *to find places—here and there—*
> *too removed from the edge of the Grass Ocean*
> *to allow the full strength of the Dark Ocean,*
> *yet devoid enough of those same trees*
> *to allow the warmth and light of Sun.*

HERE
The people encouraged seeds toward Earth.

Sites that have contained signs of early agriculture include the Phillips Spring shelter about sixty miles north of Eureka Springs and White Bluff and Eden's Bluff in Benton County, Arkansas. These sites are important because they place this area among the earliest centers in the world for agriculture. Carroll County's Blue Spring Shelter along the White River may have been a site from this period.[11] The people known as the Tom's Brook culture were one of the earliest Archaic-era peoples.[12]

A unique hunter-gatherer society, the Poverty Point culture stretched from the Gulf Coast to the junction of the Mississippi and Arkansas Rivers and had a much wider trade network, including the Ozarks. The name site in northeastern Louisiana has been recognized as a World Heritage site because it was the most elaborate mound center anywhere in the hemisphere at that time.[13]

WOODLAND

In the Arkansas Ozarks, the late Archaic and early Woodland periods are often discussed together.[14] As modern forests arose, people used upland areas, shelters and caves in the hillsides and hilltop sites, as well as lowland areas, streamside camps and villages in the valleys. They continued to have contact with neighbors in the plains to the west and the Mississippi Valley in the east.

During the Woodland period from 1000 BC to AD 1000, an increase in agriculture occurred in forests of the Northeast and Southeast. Corn appeared around AD 200. Later in the period, the Baytown and Plum Bayou cultures built mounds along the White and Arkansas Rivers, including those at the Toltec Mounds southeast of Little Rock.

As farming became central to tribal life, changing roles and power structures evolved. When hunting was primary, male societies were central so that the bonds of brothers, sons and fathers were not broken. Plant domestication was likely a result of women's gathering and encouraging seeds. As crops became a larger part of their diet, they had to stay near their fields; thus, female societies became more important. When a man married, he would move to his wife's village, and his children received their clan lineage from their mother.

Flute and other objects as found in Breckenridge Shelter, near the Beaver Dam site, close to Eureka Springs. *The University of Arkansas, Fayetteville, Museum Collections.*

With increasing use of grains, new ways of cooking and storing food became necessary, and basketry and ceramics evolved. Shell-tempered pottery was practiced in the Ozarks 100 to 150 years before it spread and was adopted in Cahokia and other Mississippian centers.

During the late Woodland period, bow-and-arrow technology became widespread. The flute, arrow shaft, turkey bone and bits of cane, gourd and squash were found in 1933 by a crew led by Sam Dellinger, likely dating from 750 to 1350 CE (common era).[15]

MISSISSIPPIAN

By AD 1000, dependence on farming had increased. Archaeologists call this late prehistoric period the Mississippian period. In the Ozarks, the geography was not suitable for large-scale farming. Small hunting, gathering and gardening communities persisted. Some sites show signs of having been task camps for working stone, hide, bone or wood. The Ozark uplands may have been sources for feathers, wood, stone or plants used in the ceremonial centers of Cahokia, near St. Louis and Spiro on the Arkansas River, just southwest of present-day Fort Smith.

Farming had become so central that evoking cooperation with nature became an art and a science. Droughts, floods, frosts, insects or animals could destroy an entire year's food supply. Individuals who could appease the negative and enlist the forces of rain, sun and moon that would bring bountiful harvests became essential.

The Corn Goddess was one of the mythological beings beseeched to bring abundant harvests. A Corn Goddess effigy pipe made between AD 1100 and 1200 out of flint clay from the Cahokia area of Illinois portrays a kneeling female figure holding cornstalks in her hands and sunflowers on her back. Cahokia at that time was the largest ceremonial center in the Mississippi Valley region, with two hundred pyramid mounds built in a five-square-mile zone.[16] The effigy pipe pictured was discovered in Desha County, Arkansas, near the mouth of the White River and the Arkansas River.

Proper burials were part of keeping balance. A mound near Huntsville, Arkansas, was built on a terrace next to War Eagle Creek. The mortuary was similar to mounds in the Caddoan area near Spiro. Its entryway was oriented toward the winter solstice sunset. According to radiocarbon dating, this site was used beginning sometime between 1256 and 1304 until the early 1400s. According to Marvin Kay, "The mound centers themselves do not appear to have been the primary place of residence for the supporting population."

Corn Goddess effigy pipe.
*Museum of Native American History,
Bentonville, Arkansas.*

By the late 1400s, the population of the Southeast was at least 155,000 and as many as 286,000. Villages were large and composed of farmsteads and plazas with temple mounds. Burial of special artifacts with the elite class may indicate hierarchical societies. The Spanish, and later the French, documented encountering societies with corn-based agriculture, populous towns, a team sport, pottery and religions centered on earth and sky gods and the morning and evening stars.

CONTACT WITH EUROPEANS

In Arkansas, first contact with Europeans was with the expedition of Hernando de Soto in 1541. In that same year, Francisco Coronado reached central Kansas, crossing the Upper Arkansas from the southwest. Contact brought the spread of European diseases, which weakened the societies and made them vulnerable, often in advance of actual encounters. De Soto died in Arkansas on May 21, 1542, and his body sunk late at night into the Mississippi River.

Rollings described the colonial period as "Living in a Graveyard."[17] Whether it was disease or drought, the large populations disappeared, and the region remained unoccupied. "The dramatic depopulation of people created a decline in hunting, and colonial Arkansas became a region filled with vast numbers of wild animals." Abundant game eventually brought Amerindian hunters and later European traders and trappers.

Chapter 3
OSAGE ENCOUNTERS

HISTORIC TRIBES

The Caddo homeland covered much of western Arkansas, eastern Oklahoma and northeast Texas. They are likely the descendants of the Mississippian people who built the mounds at Spiro. In 1542, they were invaded by the de Soto *entrada*. Besides Old World diseases, other European influences crept into Caddo society, including horses, metal tools and weapons and plants such as peaches. Caddoan reach into the Ozarks may have declined as populations shifted.

It is not known exactly when the Quapaw and Osage tribes arrived in Missouri and Arkansas. The Osages and Quapaws spoke similar languages and had similar clan structures, while the Caddo were from a different language family and an agrarian-based clan system. The Ozarks were largely unoccupied. In the fall and winter, Osage, Caddo and Quapaw hunted for deer in the highlands.[18] The Osage eventually claimed much of northwest Arkansas as their hunting grounds. The Quapaw lived in villages near the Mississippi and Arkansas Rivers, while the Caddo were pushed to the south and west.

By the time the French arrived in the late 1600s, the Osage lived in permanent villages on the Osage River, toward the northern edge of the Ozark uplands. Their villages were arranged with great care based on their history and clan structure. According to John Joseph Mathews in his book *The Osages*, "They lived at the contact line between the prairie-plains and the woodland, in a region where the Arctic air found no barriers to its savage rush and would periodically meet the dog-breath air from the Gulf to spawn disaster, which gave dramatic proof of Wah'kon, the Mystery Force."

Anyone who has been through an Ozark ice storm knows what Mathews meant. The Osage word for clan is the same as their word for fireplace.

Under the two great divisions, earth and sky, twenty-four clans—each having its own totems, guiding animals, symbols, celestial bodies or natural forces—brought order through their traditions. The family arranged marriages, and a sky clan person had to marry earth clan, and vice versa, so that the children were each part sky and part earth. The clan membership came from the father's side. Many tribal ceremonies included long songs and dances for hunting, war, peace, healing and mourning, with each clan playing a specific role.

Moving to a new country was not always a move to a new area of land; sometimes it was a new mindset or a new tradition. Choosing to have two chiefs who would rule together was one such tradition. Making the sacred hawk bundle that was for the protection of the whole tribe was another. Since prehistoric times, the wise male elders of the tribe were known as the Little Old Men.

The Osage called themselves the Little Ones, not because they had short stature—most were well over six feet tall—but rather because they thought of themselves as small as compared to the Great Mystery. They also called themselves the "Children of the Middle Waters." *Wah'Kon-Tah*, the spiritual force of the Osage, ended the *ga-ni-tha*, or chaos, by separating the middle waters, the universe in which they were to live, into the elements air, earth and water. Singing of prayers was common and could be heard morning, noon and night. A wide road went east to west through each village. The Sky People lived to the north of the road, and the Earth People lived to the south. The two chiefs lived in the center.

> *In springtime, fields were cleared along river bottoms adjacent to the village. Women from each family tended their own plots until the plants were well-enough established to be left to continue growing on their own. During the summer, residents of several villages would gather together in large camps and travel west, to Kansas and Nebraska, to hunt buffalo.* [19]

Some old women were appointed to carry weapons to protect younger women from being raped. [20]

The Little Old Men meditated about the organization of the buffalo drives. It was decided that it must be a communal effort. Scouts would be sent out to locate the herd. Then the principal chiefs, the *Tzi-Sho*, chief of the Sky People, and the *Hunkah*, chief of the Earth People, would seek a place for a hunting camp.

From the permanent village to the first camp stop, both the grand chiefs were in authority, but thereafter they alternated; one day the Tzi-Sho *was in charge and the next day the* Hunkah, *and on the last day of the return journey, when the village was the objective, both chiefs had equal authority again.*[21]

THE FRENCH PERIOD

The first individual white men to come in contact with the Osage were hunters and trappers, most likely *coureurs de bois,* French woodsmen. The Osage warriors, who were cleanshaven except for a lock of hair at the center of the head to the nape of the neck, came to call the hunters *I'n-Shta-Heh,* which meant "Heavy Eyebrows."

The French traders brought guns, hatchets, knives, scrapers, fleshers and awls, for which the Osage traded not only furs but also people. The traditional counting coup, which was a ceremonial act of bravery with their enemies such as the Pawnee, gave way to taking them alive and trading them to the French as slaves. Whole parties of Heavy Eyebrows were killed in order to keep them from trading guns with the Pawnee or other enemy tribes.[22]

La Salle and de Tonti came down the great river from the north in 1681. The entourage visited a Quapaw village, where they raised a cross and claimed the land in the name of Louis XIV. They went down the river to its mouth and claimed the entire drainage for France, calling it "Louisiana."

Henri de Tonti founded Arkansas Post in 1686. It was the first settlement in the lower Mississippi River Valley and served as a trading post, a way station for Mississippi River travel and a Jesuit mission.

The reign of Louis XIV was known for its extravagance. After he died in 1715, the country was nearly bankrupt. His great-grandson and next in line for the throne, Louis XV, was a young boy, so the Duc d'Orléans became regent. A deal was struck to bail out the Banque Royal from the revenues derived from opening the Mississippi Valley, the brainchild of Scottish financier John Law. About Law, Mathews wrote:

It was the energy of this one man who sent the first official Frenchmen to visit the chief village of the Little Ones. And it was this spirit and energy of a man far across the ocean that sent the first European cutpurses and criminals to the lower Mississippi in significant numbers, and the first Negroes, who would later come in contact with the Little Ones.

In 1716, with hope in the minds of the French that the interior of North America would be a source of riches, John Law became a national hero and was given the official title Duc d'Arkansas. He was given a twenty-five-year monopoly on trade and mineral rights, which caused a boom in company stocks and led to a riot in Paris. The prosperity was all on paper; however, a new word came into existence: "millionaire."

Commercial enterprises were turned over to the Company of the Indies, one of John Law's companies. Charles Claude du Tisne was the official visitor to meet the Osage in 1719. The Osage villages were in their post-flood positions by the time he arrived. Sometime during the early eighteenth century, a great flood had caused the river to swell and overflow. Tribal leaders decided that this was a sign to form villages in each of the five places where the people had run to escape.[23]

The groups or bands were named for the type of terrain in which they took refuge: Top-of-the-Tree-Sitters or Big Hills, Upper-Forest-Sitters or Upland-Forest People, Sitters-in-the-Locusts or Thorny-Thicket People, Down-Below-People and Heart-Stays-People. The Down-Below-People became known as the Little Osages, as to European eyes their villages seemed much different from the others. At this time, the marriages became matrilocal as well, meaning a young man would go to live with his wife's clan. The Osage tribe kept these five divisions through the colonial and territorial periods, through contact with Europeans and other tribes and through several moves to their last reservation in Oklahoma.

THE SPANISH PERIOD

In 1762, France ceded the Louisiana Territory to Spain. The transfer of Louisiana to the Spanish had been a gift from Louis XV to Charles III of Spain. French hunters were still answering to Paris, not Madrid, a year later when one of the licensees, Laclede, left New Orleans to lay the foundation for St. Louis. His assistant was fourteen-year-old Auguste Chouteau, who lived for a time with the Osage. When the Osage chieftains wanted to go to the commandant, they called St. Louis *Sho-to To-Wo'n.*

In 1793, Auguste Chouteau called on the governor general Baron de Carondelet at New Orleans and proposed to build a fort on the Osage River with his and his brother Pierre's own money if they could have exclusive rights to trade with the Great and Little Osages. The contract was signed and would run for six years, until 1800.

The Spanish never had manpower in the area to do much besides incite tension between tribes, trying to get the Quapaw to make war with the Osage. This lasted from about 1770 to 1777, when the Osage and Quapaw made peace, much to the dismay of the Spanish. East of the Mississippi, Pontiac was leading a resistance to keep the English out and go back to the old ways.

The "Mourning War" ceremony was an Osage custom of taking the scalp of the first non-Osage a mourning party found in order to retaliate for the death of an Osage. Enough whites were killed in this way that the Spaniards wanted to cut off trade with the tribe. During the Spanish era, a faction broke away from the tribe and established itself on the Upper Arkansas River. These Arkansas Osage, often younger men who could not be controlled by the larger tribal authorities, were often responsible for killings of European and Indian hunters on the Arkansas, White and St. Francis Rivers.[24]

CARVING THE BASIN

The main artifact showing that Indians were at Eureka Springs is the basin in the rock itself. About the size of a washbasin, the carved hole exists in the rock in a crawl space under the cement semicircle of Basin Park.

A letter dated May 18, 1884, from Colonel John M. Richardson, a lawyer from Carthage, Missouri, to former Arkansas governor Powell Clayton has been claimed as proof that Indians considered the site a sacred place and used the waters for healing. The text, published in Johnston's 1884 guide to Eureka Springs, was republished many times and has become part of the traditional history of the town:

> *Dear Sir: It was in the summer of 1847 when a conversation took place between White Hair, principle chief of the Great and Little Osage Indians, and myself at the office of the agency, on Rock Creek [now Kansas], relative to lead in Missouri, and a celebrated spring in the mountains. The chief said when he was a boy the Osages took lead out of the bottom of the creek and smelted it with dry bark, and then run it into bullets. He stated that where the lead was found was in the prairie and in Missouri, and two days' travel from the place in the mountains was a spring the Indians visited for the purpose of using the waters and getting cured. He said he never knew an Indian "go there with sore eyes and drink the water and wash in it for a whole moon but what was cured."*

Close-up of Basin Spring's famous basin, 1879.

The chief said Black Dog's father, when a boy, scoured out a smooth hole in the rock out of which they would dip water with cups; that the hole was about the size of the tin basins the white people washed in. The Indians, supposing the spirit of the great Medicine Man hovered round the spring, never camped near it, and never had any fighting near it. In considering Black Dog's age, I conclude the basin was scoured out seventy years previous to the conversation. The chief said the water spread out over the rock and the hole was scoured in the rock to concentrate the water, and at times it was used to pound corn in to make meal, and that I would know the spring by the hole in the rock. The circumstance had entirely faded from my memory, but in visiting Eureka Springs in 1880, the conversation with the chief recurred to my mind. I felt sure that was the great Indian spring.

Very truly,
J.M. Richardson.

The name of Black Dog's father remains a mystery. A leader of part of the tribe that would become known as the Black Dog band, Black Dog's father located to the region called the Little Ozarks near Baxter Springs, Kansas, possibly as early as 1775, according to Louis Burns in *A History of the Osage People*. Black Dog was born around 1780. His father died when he was sixteen years old. The name *Manka Chonkeh*, Black Dog, was given to him by his companions after he silenced a barking dog with an arrow from the darkness while on a raid against the Comanche.[25] Black Dog, who died on March 24, 1848, was chief at the time White Hair related the story of the spring to Colonel Richardson. Black Dog II later succeeded his father and led the band into the twentieth century.

The Osage had survived the French colonial period, made peace with tribes influenced by Spanish intrigue and managed to adapt to many changes brought about by the whites. They had begun to depend on European goods and had learned to place them in context with their own traditions. During the 1790s, the Osage nation was large, with 1,200 to 1,500 warriors. Engaging in warfare with other tribes to control their claim to hunting grounds and to prevent sales of guns and ammunition to their enemies, they roamed from the Missouri River in the north to the Red River in the south. They traded more furs and skins than any tribe in the territory.[26]

The tide changed when Louisiana became property of the United States in 1803. President Jefferson assigned the task of negotiating with the Osage to Pierre Chouteau, the agent of Indian affairs for the Louisiana Territory. In exchange for the safe passage for government expeditions on the rivers through their territory, they would be provided with a blacksmith, a mill and tools and equipment such as plows. These civilizing influences were resisted by the Osage, whose concerns were wars with their enemies on the plains and in the woodlands.

William Dunbar and Dr. George Hunter led an expedition up the Ouachita River in the fall of 1804 to Hot Springs, Arkansas. "The president had heard of the hot springs from a friend in Natchez, Mississippi—William Dunbar, a planter and amateur scientist. Jefferson asked Dunbar to lead an expedition into the Ouachita Mountains and report on the Indian tribes, minerals, flora and fauna, and the legendary hot springs."[27] Hunter, a chemist, analyzed the spring water. Hot Springs was set aside as a reservation by Congress in 1832.

The massacre of an undefended Osage village in 1805 by Potawatomi raiders marked a critical change in the Osage. Thirty-four women and children were killed, and sixty captives were taken, but the Osage did not retaliate.

Chapter 4

LONG HUNTERS

B efore there were political boundaries in an area, the lay of the land was understood by its rivers and streams. The best sources of information on the true nature of new lands were hunters who could describe the terrain. While primarily after furs, they were invaluable to settlers who sought to cross the Appalachians and move farther west. Long hunters, who ventured for years at a time, located the best routes for travel and the most suitable land for settlement and identified springs for drinking water and for salt. Sometimes they were financed by land speculators who paid for detailed information.

Among the long hunters, whose descendants live in the Eureka Springs area today, were William Vaughan and his daughter Sally's husband, Phillip Harp. Cora Pinkley-Call's great-grandmother, Molly Vaughan Stone, and grandmother, Nancy Vaughan Harp, as well as June Westphal's ancestors, John Lewis Harp and Lucy Vaughan Harp, descend from these explorers. According to these families, tales of a great healing spring were an important part of the traditions that brought them to the Ozarks highland area in Arkansas Territory.

Cora Pinkley was born in 1892, the youngest of ten children. When she was just a baby, her uncle Benjamin Vaughan petitioned the Cherokee to be included as a tribal member. Her great uncle, Absalom Harp, sought to qualify for land in Indian Territory. They believed themselves to be part Cherokee, a lineage going back to before the American Revolution.

A Wilderness Wedding

There are written accounts of a William Vaughan who traded fur pelts in the western Virginia region as early as 1718, and this could be the same William Patrick Vaughan who died before 1800 and is believed to be buried, along with his Cherokee wife, Fair-as-the-Moon, in Sweeten's Cove in Marion County, Tennessee. The family believes that they were married in a traditional Cherokee way.

In pre–Revolutionary War times, mating ceremonies were long and could last up to four moons. The shaman would have instructed the bride and groom. In one tale, the Corn Goddess was sent by the Star People to teach individuals about food medicine. The strawberry grew in the shape of a heart and could be helpful in bringing harmony to intimate relationships.[28]

During the ceremony, the bride and groom came to the sacred circle in their bare feet, better to hear Mother Earth's heartbeat. Cornmeal was

Early 1880s view of the White River Valley from Cedar Bluff, Beaver, Arkansas.

added to the circle in a counterclockwise direction. The shaman would bring tobacco to add to the circle, walking around seven times, one for each of the Cherokee clans.

It was among the Cherokee that Old William Vaughan heard the stories of a Great Indian Healing Spring on the other side of the Mississippi. He and Philip Harp set out from Kentucky to explore this land that was said to be a hunter's paradise.

Following Indian traces into what is now northwest Arkansas, they heard many stories about a spring that could cure "fire in the bone" (rheumatism) and blindness. It was said that although the Osage Indians were hostile to the Cherokee and many other tribes, they let them bring their sick to the spring. The water was thought to cure by drawing fire out of the flint rocks through which it passed.

CUMBERLAND GAP

William Patrick and Fair-as-the-Moon had a son, William, who was born around 1750. The story takes up with him. By the time he came of age, he had learned a great deal about life in the wilderness as a trader, trapper and explorer.

William found the girl who was to be his wife among the Native Americans somewhere in the tree-covered mountains in the western part of the old North Carolina Colony. Her name was Fereby Benton, a very English-sounding name, but many Cherokee Indians had very early on adopted the names used by those first colonists from Great Britain. The couple's firstborn, Thomas, came about 1773. At this time, the family was paying 10 percent of their annual proceeds in taxes, appearing in the "tithables" list for the New River country, west of Roanoke, Virginia.

Lord Dunmore, governor of Virginia, ordered the frontier to fortify itself from the Shawnee and their allies, the Mingos, who claimed that valley. Rather than wait for attack, the Holston Militia marched down the New River to its mouth on the Ohio. The Battle of Point Pleasant in 1774 showed the settlers that they could indeed fend off the Indians. William Vaughan served in Captain David Looney's Company. He, along with Captain Looney, Lieutenant Daniel Boone and Lieutenant John Cox, guarded the Clinch frontier. During the Revolution itself, it is believed that William, his wife and their three young sons lived in the wilderness with the Cherokee.[29]

The family settled in Russell County, Virginia, in 1783. Daniel was born four years later and named for his father's friend and fellow adventurer

Daniel Boone. When William and Fereby removed their household and family from Virginia to a new home on Little War Creek, Hawkins County, it was shortly after Tennessee had become the sixteenth state in 1796. It was a large family of at least ten sons and daughters, one of them being Louisa, called "Lucy," who would later marry John Louis Harp. Son Samuel, just turned twenty-one, was still at home, as he was yet unmarried.

COUNTRY OF THE SIX BULLS

Long hunters have proved to be an invaluable source of information about the interior of the continent. Such information about the West came from a long hunter who may have spent fifteen years among the Indians beyond the Mississippi. Edmund Jennings was born in Bedford, Virginia, in 1751. He was in the Battle of Point Pleasant and was among the axemen who opened the Wilderness Trail from Long Island of the Holston River to Otter Creek, Kentucky. He was among the veterans who got a land grant along the Cumberland River in Davidson County, Tennessee, in 1783. His father, Jonathan, was killed by Indians the next year, and Jennings, taking his long rifle, disappeared into the forest.

John C. Cox was a youth in Middle Tennessee when he heard a firsthand description of the White River region from Edmund Jennings:

> *On foot and alone he found his way into this region, and for fifteen years lived on peaceable terms with the Indians, isolated from civilization, and spending his time in hunting, trapping, and fishing. His friends in Tennessee gave him up for dead…One day, however, to the great surprise of the community among which he had formerly lived, he returned, dressed in skins and moccasins, and so unused to the English tongue that it was with difficulty he could make himself understood…He stated, that he had been in the far west in the "Country of the Six Boils"…His pronunciation of the word "boils" was so corrupt that his listeners first conceived it to be "bulls," but the old pioneer explained that he referred by the term to six boiling, bubbling streams of water that traversed his favorite region, and along whose banks for long years he had trapped and hunted. He doubtless alluded to the Cow Skin, Indian Creek, Shoal Creek, Centre Creek, Spring River and North fork.[30]*

According to some sources, the six boils referred to the six great springs that feed a number of creeks and rivers in the Ozarks. Word of the good waters, abundant game and healthfulness of the land spread and triggered a rush of settlers to the area now known as southwest Missouri.

Upon his return to Tennessee, Jennings ran a ferry service along the Cumberland River at Jennings Creek. A license was granted to run the ferry in 1799. Rates were established as follows: "For man and horse, 18 1/3 cents; single man and single horse, each 9 cents; wagon and team, $1.25; cattle, hogs and sheep, 6¼ cents each." Jennings passed away in 1840, which happens to be the time the Alvah Jackson family came from Allen County, Kentucky, adjacent to Jennings's home in Tennessee, into Barry County, Missouri.

REMOVALS: SETTLERS AND INDIANS

Daniel Vaughan sold his land on the Caney River in White County, Tennessee, in 1816 and headed west. William and Fereby followed after their daughter Lucy married John Lewis Harp and was settled in Warren County, Tennessee.

In 1825, the chief who was the leader of the local group signed a treaty, along with many other Osage chiefs and warriors, giving up their Arkansas lands to the United States. *Hurachais* (War Eagle) "touched the feather," signing a mark on the document and signaling the end of their claim to these lands. War Eagle Creek bears his name.[31]

On May 6, 1828, Cherokee Indians signed a treaty giving up their Arkansas lands for a new home in what later became Oklahoma. This led to a split in the tribe as one group moved to Oklahoma and others tried to remain; some even went to Missouri.[32]

The sheriff census of Washington County, Arkansas, in 1829 noted the arrival of new settlers. These included Samuel Vaughan and his wife, Catherine Hammons; Daniel Vaughan and his wife, Margaret Hammons; and William and Fereby Benton Vaughan and their grandson Benjamin, as well as John and Louisa "Lucy" Vaughan Harp and their children, Hardy, Absolom, Tolbert, Lewis and James. The traditional family history passed down from generation to generation from their long hunter ancestors had brought them to the lands of the Great Healing Spring.

Chapter 5

PIONEER LIFEWAYS

A lvah Jackson, a pioneer doctor, recognized the medicinal value of the water, and by the 1880s, he was a legendary figure. Later, he was painted as either a hero or a quack; two vastly different histories emerged. In one, he was born in Georgia, and in another he was an immigrant from England. Both may provide insights into his life and times. Either way, it was not an easy journey, and medicine had little to offer in the form of relief.

A COLONIAL PATHWAY

The family history in which Alvah Jackson was born in Georgia may extend back to Nottinghamshire, England, in the 1600s. A genetic test on the Y chromosome of a Jackson cousin pointed to a shared ancestor in a colonial family on Long Island at that time. Further DNA testing may show that the Jacksons of Carroll County are part of this very large branch on the genetic tree.

Jim Hinkle of Missouri, while researching his own family tree, discovered that Alvah Jackson's father was William R. Jackson, born in 1769 or 1770 in Orange County, North Carolina, and died in Allen County, Kentucky, around 1824. A letter from his granddaughter Susan B. Jackson Hendrick described him:

> *He was a tall six footer of fair complexion, a deacon in the Baptist Church. He had a brother, Benjamin, who was a preacher in the Primitive Baptist Church. Also a cousin, Howard Jackson (Benjamin's son), also a*

Baptist Minister. Grandfather moved to Allen County, Kentucky, near Russellville and spent his last days there. I was born January 7, 1837 in Allen County, Kentucky.

From Cane Creek in North Carolina, the brothers William and Benjamin moved to the Pendleton District in western South Carolina. By 1794, he had found a wife, Mary Humphries, and lived in northeast Georgia. Elijah and Franklin were born, and by 1797, Mary had died. William remarried Nancy Terrell Jackson and had sons William R. and Stephen. After a break of a few years, she had one baby a year for the next five years: Moses Terrell, Alvah, Nancy, Wiseman and Benjamin.

In 1805, Georgia began distributing land formerly belonging to the Creek and Cherokee Indians through a series of lotteries. William may have felt that it was time to remove his family to a safer and healthier location. In 1810, his name appeared on the census of Warren County, Kentucky. News of the expeditions of Lewis and Clark, Zebulin Pike, Dunbar and Hunter in the lands west of the Mississippi had begun to circulate by this time. As Alvah was growing up on one frontier, others opened beyond. Many Revolutionary War veterans and other settlers had populated the Cumberland River area around Nashville. Allen County, Kentucky, was just north of that area.

In 1818, Millie was born in Allen County, Kentucky, and two years later July Ann, or "Juley," arrived. Tax lists from 1815 to 1823 show variations of the name R. William or William R. or just William. The next year, Nancy Jackson's name is associated with the 250 acres that had been taxed for the preceding years under her husband's name.

On October 20, 1828, Alvah Jackson and Nancy Elizabeth Coleman were married by John Howard in Allen County. Nancy's father was Captain Jeremiah "William" Coleman. Little is known of her background except that she had a younger sister, Lucy. Two sons were born, William F. in 1830 and Thomas Berry in 1831.

Alvah must have been a very upstanding young man. Perhaps his mother was a victim of the cholera epidemic that spread through Kentucky during the summer of 1833. In October 1833, he was assigned guardianship of his sisters after fifteen-year-old Millie and thirteen-year-old Juley appeared in court and chose him to take that responsibility. Around that same time, his third son, John Franklin, was born.

Doctors were often called upon to be officers of the law. In December 1835, Alvah Jackson was appointed constable. He may also have received medical training prior to this period. In a statement in 1880, he signed that he was a graduate of Douglas Medical School of Kentucky. In 1837 and 1840, two more daughters, Lucy and Mary, respectively, were added to the family.

It is likely that the family moved overland from Allen County, Kentucky, and crossed the Mississippi at one of the usual crossings after their baby was born in 1840 and Nancy was able to travel. The journey would have taken six weeks to two months. However, stopovers to the homes of cousins and siblings who had moved earlier to Boone and Camden Counties in central Missouri would have been likely. By 1841, Alvah Jackson was a justice of the peace in Barry County, Missouri, which included today's Barry, Lawrence, Dade, McDonald, Newton, Jasper, Barton and a part of Cedar County. Court records showed that Alvah Jackson performed two weddings: on October 14, 1841, James D. Bonner and Elizabeth A. Gibson, and on November 16, 1841, George Gossage and Lucy Coleman, Nancy Jackson's sister.

The Jacksons had four more children born after they moved to Arkansas: Larkin, Nancy J., James H. and Juliann. According to the 1850 U.S. census of Carroll County, Alvah Jackson was a forty-three-year-old mechanic from Georgia. During the industrial age, "mechanic" came to mean any of a number of skilled workers. A mechanical physiologist was one who used mechanical theories like those of Isaac Newton to understand the workings of the body. Jackson's three oldest sons were listed as farmers.

An old church record from the Rock Springs Baptist Church included Alvah Jackson and his wife, who were lettered from a Baptist church in Olin (Allen) County, Kentucky. It was 1853, and the Jacksons, along with a small group of pioneer Christians, met in a cabin near the Kings River in Carroll County, about halfway between present-day Berryville and Eureka Springs.[33]

FAMILY TRADITIONAL HISTORY

A very different history of Dr. Jackson was provided by one of his descendants. The following was a footnote in Alice Baker Gentry's article about Rock Springs Church in the *Arkansas Historical Quarterly* in the winter of 1947:

> *Dr. Alva Jackson was a full blooded Englishman who came directly from London—a graduate of Oxford College—and M.D. and a surgeon. He first practiced in New Orleans. Practiced there in a hospital a few years then migrated up the Mississippi and finally located at Paducah, Kentucky. There he married Nancy Coleman (a Dutch girl). They had nine children—five*

boys and four girls. He taught all of them to read, write and "figger" (as it was then called—the 3 R's). He gave Uncle John, the doctor, an education. During the thirties he built a flatboat and brought his family to Arkansas. They traveled down the Ohio and Mississippi river to the mouth of the Arkansas; up White river to King's river, thence up that stream to their future home. Dr. Alva brought his medicine books and instruments from England with him. He regularly sent back to England for medicine. Also he shipped, via New Orleans to England, bear pelts, bear oil, and many native plants, among them, Mayapple, Gensing and Wahoo.—This information has been obtained from his great-granddaughter (his oldest living descendant) Mrs. Maude (Boswell) Black, Harrison, Arkansas.

A young medical student looks across the harbor at the clipper ships unloading cotton to be turned into textiles in the bustling British factories. He dreams of life on the American frontier. What would it be like to explore the wilderness like Lewis and Clark? A young aristocrat may have had to go against his parents to fulfill his dream. Once arriving in New Orleans, he is put to work right away. The hospital is filled with patients needing attention. He quickly learns the reality behind the cotton bales that romantically called him to this destiny. The price of cotton is directly tied to the going rate for a slave.

After a few years in the port, he decides to go up the mighty river into the heart of the continent. There he finds a brand-new town called Paducah, Kentucky. Now the market is bustling with activity and new opportunities. Just two years before, a community of white settlers and Indians had been living peacefully side by side when the famous explorer, now Indian agent, William Clark told them to move on because he was going to build a planned city on that site.

The doctor falls for a woman and asks for her hand in marriage, and she agrees. She also agrees to leave this outpost on the junctions of several great rivers to find a remote spot farther in the wilderness. On the way there, they stop off in Oil Trough in Arkansas Territory, where a booming bear oil trade is employing at least twenty-five men. The enterprise lasts for only five years before the bears are all gone.[34] Finally, they reach their spot of paradise and settle down to the business of having children and grandchildren. This scenario may be missing support, yet it sheds light on some of the tragic realities of pioneer life in the 1820s and '30s.

REDISCOVERING THE SPRING

From the hilltops around Alvah Jackson's homestead, he could see the tree-topped mountains that enclosed the area his family had chosen to settle. To the west was largely uninhabited wilderness; to the east across the Kings River was a small settlement, the town of Berryville.

While there were few slaveholding families in the rural area, news of the dark cloud of impending war forming in Kansas may have been on Alvah's mind as he roamed the woods that day with his dogs. His three older sons had reached majority and were putting in crops. Larkin, the first in the family to be born in Arkansas, was now in his teens. What would a war do to their family? Praying that God's bounty would continue to smile on them, he heard the dogs barking and the hiss and scream of a wildcat.

I, Alva Jackson, of Carroll county and State of Arkansas, do hereby certify that the following statement of my discovery of Eureka Springs, in the county of Carroll and State of Arkansas and on the head of Leatherwood, one of the tributaries of White River, is in all the particulars true and correct:[35]

About twenty-four years ago I was hunting bear at the head of Leatherwood. About 10 o'clock, my dogs, three in number, started in and run a panther into a hole in the cliff, about thirty yards above the spring. I came up to them in a few minutes and found the dogs and panther engaged in a terrible fight in the hole clear out of sight. About two o'clock the fight ended by my dogs killing the panther. I was present within a few feet all the time the fight was going on, though I could not get a chance to help them in the fight—the hole being too small. Two of my dogs came out torn so badly that I had no hopes of their recovery.

Before the dogs came out I could hear them pulling at the panther as if they were trying to pull him out of the hole. They left the other dog in the hole behind the panther. There were large, heavy rocks in the hole that I could not get out without help, so I returned home, but came back the next morning with my son, William, and seven other persons. My son had sore eyes at the time, and he complained that he did not feel like work; therefore, I advised him to wash his eyes in the spring, for I had believed for a long time that there were some medical properties in the spring. He did so for some three times during our stay at the spring. We finally relieved my dog and found him badly torn by the panther. The panther was jammed in a small hole in the cliff so close that I could not get him out. So I left him there and went home.

The next morning you could not have told my son ever had sore eyes. His eyes were completely cured, and this convinced me that there was medical virtue in the water. I had read the history of the Spanish adventurer, Ponce De Leon, and other histories of this section of the country, in which they spoke of a spring being somewhere in this region that performed great cures, at least so the Indians reported. They also reported that they even strangely improved, and that there was virtue in the water. I went back the third day to further examine the spring. I went to work cleaning away dirt and rock, and after a time I discovered a hole or Basin in the rock. It was full of blue mud. Found flint and gravel packed so close and hard that it was very troublesome to dig out. I had to use a common crowbar to dig the mud and gravel out.

When I had cleaned and washed the basin out and examined it thoroughly, I felt fully satisfied that I had found it. And having used and tested that water fully for twenty-four years, I am convinced, in my own mind, it is the spring spoken of by the Spanish discoverer of this country.

I am a graduate of the Douglas Medical School of Kentucky,
[Signed] *ALVA JACKSON*

If Jackson penned this statement during the last months of his life, then his discovery occurred around 1856.

After the healing of his son's eye ailment, Jackson began using water from the spring in his practice. "Having thoroughly satisfied himself of the efficacy of the water in such cases, the Doctor extended his practice in this direction. 'Dr. Jackson's eye-water' acquired a wide reputation in this and adjoining States."[36]

WAR AND ITS AFTERMATH

The Civil War brought devastation to the region along the Arkansas-Missouri border. After the major battle in the vicinity at Pea Ridge in March 1862, the hills became a no-man's land.

According to numerous official communications the area of the upper White River watershed was practically depopulated near the end of hostilities. The people of both Union and Confederate sympathies were either killed or had to move out, going north or south depending upon where their loyalties lay. The guerrilla forces of both sides had to limit their activities because there was little left to subsist on. The fields and the farms were deserted.

There were but few homes left standing to return to should anyone have thought of returning.[37]

According to historian Goodspeed, "Dr. Jackson was frequently called upon by the sick and wounded of both armies." He set up a hospital under a ledge near the basin-shaped spring. Among those treated at the spring was Major J.W. Cooper, of Cooper's battalion, in the Cherokee brigade of the Confederate army.

This officer contracted rheumatism and chronic malarial poison while campaigning in the Southwest, and having obtained leave of absence, he came to Dr. Jackson, in February, 1865. As this section was then occupied by the Federals it became necessary to take refuge in the mountain fastnesses; and a party, consisting of the Doctor, the Major, William Nichols, Sine Creeley, and two others, took refuge in the "rock house," near the present site of the Southern Hotel. Here they lived in archaic simplicity, and in a few months the soldiers had completely recovered.[38]

Reunion, in February 1880, of Dr. Jackson, Major Cooper and other soldiers the doctor treated during the Civil War.

As people returned after the war, they began the difficult task of rebuilding. Dr. Jackson's neighbors, brothers Ephraim and Absolm Thomas, one a Confederate and the other a Union man, were reunited and eventually were laid to rest side by side at the Bunch Cemetery.

When a Confederate veteran, Isaac Clarke, returned from Indian Territory in October 1865, he was saddened by the miserable conditions he found.[39] Carrollton, Berryville and Huntsville were nearly burned to the ground. After seeking other options to no avail, Clarke finally decided to open a boarding school where he would teach English, Latin and Greek. He purchased a partially built house on property outside Berryville and finished the construction. His mother served as matron, looking out for the daily welfare of the students. Like other area residents, they were putting their lives back together.

Ex-Confederate soldiers were disenfranchised, and Negros gained voting rights. General Powell Clayton became governor in July 1868, and in his first address to the legislature, he asked people to set aside their differences and work toward the good of the state. Soon, the requirements for readmittance were met, and Arkansas was accepted into the Union.

Much of the state was besieged by vigilante violence, including an estimated two hundred murders during the three months leading up to the November 3, 1868 national elections.[40] The day after the election, Governor Clayton declared martial law in ten counties; later, another four were added, of which only Conway and Fulton Counties were near the Ozarks.

Chapter 6

THE CATALYST

The people of Carroll County were self-reliant, consuming local products and trading with the outside only when goods could not be found within the area. Sometimes a whole family would take a week off and make the six-day, hundred-mile trip via wagon track to Springfield, Missouri, and back. Wool and cotton were traded for "city" goods, such as salt, coffee, ammunition and tools. In 1867, the Saunders family moved to Carroll County in order to enroll their children in the Clarke Academy. Two of the Saunderses' children, Missouri and Buck, were among ninety-two students in the school session of September 1870. Judge Saunders built a home and opened a store on what is now the Berryville square.

Levi Best Saunders was born on December 25, 1816, in Richmond, Virginia. His wife, Martha Sherrod, born on May 18, 1820, came to Madison County, Arkansas, from Maury County, Tennessee. They had six daughters and then a son. The family tried their hand at ranching in northwest Texas near Greenville. They decided to return to Washington County after an incident in which Martha and one of her daughters were kidnapped by Indians. In the rescue attempt, Saunders's partner was killed.

Saunders suffered from an ulcer on his leg that had defied the attempts of several physicians to treat it. His testimony of the cure appeared in *Joy to the Afflicted* in 1882:[41]

> *During the summer of 1878 I was troubled with the erysipelas and a good surplus of flesh—could scarcely drag myself about, and was in no condition to attend to business of any kind. In May 1879 I was connected in business with Rev. Baker, who advised me to go to Tom Thumb and Rock springs for my health, as I was not improving under medical treatment. I*

told him I was acquainted with the character of those springs—that they were common sulphur springs, and would do me no good. After a pause he told me that Bro. Alva Jackson had been telling him that there was a spring some six or eight miles west of his [Jackson's] house, in the pine hills, that he thought had some medical properties. He had also told him of some cures, made by the springs, of sore eyes and old sores. Bro. Jackson had also told him there were a couple of basins cut in the rock at the springs, one of which was as nice and smooth as any earthen basin he had ever washed from, and that it would hold about a bucket of water.

Upon learning about the basin, Saunders remembered hearing stories of a healing spring at least twice in his life prior to moving to the area:

The very moment he mentioned those basins I remembered the information received from the Indian and Spaniard, and turning to my wife, I mentioned that the basins were some signs of the Great Healing Springs, and that I would get Dr. Jackson to take me to the springs so that I could see them for myself.

Forty years had passed since he first heard about a great healing spring on a tributary of the White River while visiting with an "old settler" among the Cherokee in Indian Territory. The Indian had said that "he believed that its waters would heal any disease of the human family that the Big Owl–Great Spirit ever intended to be healed." At age sixty-one, he thought about another time in his younger days when an old Spaniard had asked him if anyone had yet discovered the "Great World Healing Spring," and he wished he had asked more questions. His testimony went on to say:

The next morning I went to Dr. Jackson's and he told me the same story. Owning to some church business that he had to attend to, he could not go with me until the next day. He invited me to remain with him all night, which invitation I accepted.

The next morning, Dr. Jackson, Levi Saunders and Buck Saunders took off from the Jackson homestead. They made their way along roads until there were no more and then through the forest to the spring, which was located about halfway down the opposite side of the mountain.

On the morrow we went to the spring and I found it as represented. Basin and all. Dr. Jackson asked me what I thought of the spring. I answered that

I thought well enough to try it for myself, fully believing then, as now, that it was the Great World Healing Springs of which I had been told.

After a few days, the judge told his son that he believed his leg was healing and that he would like to stay for a while longer. Buck left his father and returned home. According to Buck, he brought his mother to the camp by buggy on her birthday, May 18, 1879. In order to get his mother down the steep hillside, he brought the buggy to the edge of East Mountain, cut a small tree, tied it to the back of the buggy, roped the rear wheels securely to the tree and, with the back wheels locked, slid the "hack" down the mountainside.[42]

Later, Buck took his team to Massman's mill, which was five miles below the camp. He brought back lumber to build a small shack:

The sides were formed of poles dove-tailed together at the corners, and the roof consisted of rough boards. The first team was driven to the vicinity of Basin Spring by Burton Sanders, son of the judge. The first occupants of the first house were two lady members of his family.[43]

Saunders lost weight and felt totally renewed in his time at the spring:

In five weeks I lost thirty-three pounds in weight—by the scales, and forty odd pounds during my stay, but felt as if I had been thoroughly renovated or made anew, and am now, as I ever was in my life. I will also add, from the frequent bathing of my head in the waters and the improved condition of my health, portions of my hair changed from a yellowish white to a black—its original color. The color of the hair then grown was not changed, but a new crop grew out from the scalp, of the color of my hair in the younger days.

The National Holiday

The second family to arrive at the spring was that of Squire John Whitson, a friend of Judge Saunders. In this time before telephones, word spread by way of the grapevine, one person to another and very quickly. The previous summer had been disastrous for the Mississippi Valley; an epidemic of yellow fever had swept through from New Orleans to Memphis and on up, taking as many as twenty thousand lives. Many people would have been ready to jump at the chance to find a healthier locale.

By Independence Day, a growing crowd was gathered around the little spring:

> *On the Fourth of July in 1879 there were twenty families camped here. Dr. Jackson had ridden over for more water and to visit with Saunders.*
>
> *Judge Saunders said, "Doctor, people are beginning to come here, and the first thing you know there will be a town, so we had better name it."*
>
> *Dr. Jackson said, "We will call it Saunders Springs."*
>
> *"No," Judge Saunders said, "we will call it Jackson Springs."*
>
> *But neither could agree. Burton, who was listening, and who only a few days before had been reading of Ponce de Leon and his hunt for the fountain of youth, said, "Let's call it 'Eureka' meaning 'I have found it,'" and thus Eureka Springs was named.*

A film of the naming of Eureka Springs was made by Jerry Moore in 1946, based on a script by Cora Pinkley-Call, with descendants of the original settlers playing the parts. After its one and only viewing at the Crescent Hotel, C.B. Saunders told the filmmaker, "That's just how it was."

Covered wagons, leveled as well as they could be on the steep hillsides, became temporary homes. Tents were pitched. Others followed the Saunderses' lead and built themselves small shacks.

The encampment, circa 1879.

THE NEXT GENERATION

After graduating from the Clarke Academy, Buck Saunders went on to study business at a school in St. Louis. He could have settled down in his job at the brand-new Bank of Eureka Springs upon his return, but he had already developed a sense of adventure. Upon his Granddaddy Sherrod's knee, he had learned to shoot a muzzleloader at age four. He could hunt so well by the time he was a teenager that he got the nickname "Buck." His given name was Charles Burton Saunders. By age twenty-five, he was a deputy U.S. marshal. He became a marksman with the Buffalo Bill show, putting on shooting exhibits with Annie Oakley. He traveled extensively and collected guns and other rare items, many of which are in the Saunders Museum in Berryville.

Missouri Saunders was likely one of the two female members of the family living in the first slab house built near the spring and was probably present on that Fourth of July. While a student at the Clarke Academy, she met J.C. Hanna, a young man from Fayetteville. He then studied at the University of Arkansas and entered the mercantile business. By 1882, the couple had three young children. Her father had passed away in 1881, and they removed their family to Spokane Falls, Washington Territory.

In Washington, a fierce campaign for women's right to vote had been raging for about a decade, and in 1883, the Woman's Suffrage Act was passed into law. Missouri's husband died in a tragic accident. The single mother became a businesswoman in real estate and home building.

Then her young daughter, Mercie, was injured in a bicycle accident. Her son, Kirke, age nineteen, died after taking morphine for a bowel obstruction. In 1904, she moved to Edmonds hoping that the sea air and salt might benefit her invalid daughter. There she continued in property development and tried her hand at publishing. Outraged that her rights were being eroded as the territory approached statehood, she became a suffragette and the first female newspaper publisher in Washington. When she died in 1926, Missouri T.B. Hanna was known as the "Mother of Journalism."

Chapter 7

CAMP TO CITY

Tall pines towered over the Eureka Springs; clear water trickled around the basin while family members took care of their sick, the scent of cooking fires in the air. At that time, places were thought to be imbued with health or sickness, and the campers believed that they had found the former. A source of spiritual comfort, sweet water flowed to quench the thirst of body and soul. "Springs reassured grime-encrusted, mosquito-bitten travelers that their God had endowed the world judiciously with resource as well as threat."[44]

O.D. Thornton lived east of camp near the town of Berryville in Pleasant Valley. He saw the need to provide food and supplies to the growing band of invalids. He unhitched his wagon and began selling his wares. On July 6, he built a little shanty, becoming the town's first dealer in general merchandise and groceries. Soon, the ladies came to buy his calico cloth, and Thornton cut the yardage for them with his pocketknife.[45]

Like Thornton, others in nearby communities saw the rapid influx of health seekers as an opportunity. In 1879, there were 120 "working oxen" in the county.[46] Teams of oxen were the best way to carry heavy loads, fording streams, climbing hills and avoiding stumps and boulders; however, getting down the other side often proved the biggest challenge. Tolbert Harp lived in Williams Hollow near Keel's Creek and used his team of four to six oxen to haul lumber for Mrs. Massman's Mill.

Charley Birk hauled pine knots and sold them to campers for firewood for fifty cents a wagonload. Mr. and Mrs. Charles Hussey brought the first load of lumber hauled down over the extremely steep East Mountain Road into the campsite. Local farmers brought in food. "They came from miles and miles, driving their geese, ducks and turkeys on foot…Eggs were packed in wagon loads, using hay between the layers—as we pack potatoes or apples."[47]

Eureka Springs,
circa 1880.
*Courtesy Shiloh
Museum of
Ozark History/
Lockwood W.
Searcy Collection
(S-77-66-24).*

"Egg Seller," 1880.

Men began clearing trees and brush in the valley below along the dry creek bed. Soon, buildings went up on either side of the road called Main Street. Wagon traffic along the road, dusty or muddy in turn, was worsened as heavy rains ran down the valley and could turn into a torrent. Main Street later earned the nickname "Mud Street."

The basin became a gathering place as campers came to "take the water" for healing. A public meeting was held, and the first town committee was selected to take care of practical matters of the burgeoning community. Hugh Montgomery, T. Montgomery, Jacob Mills, Q. Bennett, J. Hooker, Alderson, McGuire, Nuby, Hardin, Tatum, Cook and another were the original committee of twelve. Their first order of business was to appoint a surveyor who would designate a reservation of one hundred feet around Basin Spring.

Isaac Newton Armstrong, or Major Armstrong, from Benton County, was appointed as surveyor. He started at the Great Basin Spring, setting off a reservation around the spring, and then an avenue sixty feet wide to the intersection of Main Street was surveyed. Mr. Thornton paid the first dollar for the first forty- by forty-foot lot, Number 1. According to one source, the men were measuring the site to the south of the basin that would become the Southern Hotel when a tragic accident occurred in the camp.

Early Basin Spring with the Southern Hotel, winter 1879–80.

Professor Isaac Clarke, with his wife and family, had come to relax by the spring. They were no doubt curious about what was going on at the new spa just twelve miles from their home. As they were having lunch at their camp on August 8, a tree that had a fire burning at its base fell on Virginia Layton Clarke and the baby in her arms. The baby was unharmed, but Mrs. Clarke was badly injured and died. Professor Clarke continued to visit Eureka Springs for many years on the anniversary of his wife's death, as though her spirit remained part of the community.

Weary travelers felt a sense of relief when they finally arrived at the springs. From any direction, it was a torturous journey. The nearest train depot was fifty-five miles away, in Pierce City, Missouri. Determined to get to the springs, some passengers hired "hacks" from liverymen. They loaded up with provisions and made their way, fording numerous streams and climbing and descending hill after hill. Eventually, liverymen from Eureka met the trains and provided transport.

Thomas Berry Jackson built the first bathhouse near Basin Spring. Dr. Alvah Jackson had settled on the Kings River when Thomas was ten years old. Thomas and his wife, Eliza Jane, had been married nearly thirty years and were grandparents of three. They had been farmers and perhaps had even helped Dr. Jackson with his Civil War hospital.

They may have wanted to be part of the phenomenal events at the spring because of her traditional history as well as his. Her ancestors, the Matlocks, had left the old family spring on the border between Wales and Britain around the time of the American Revolution. According to a legend told by members of a branch of the family that went to Oregon, their ancestors were driven from Matlock Spring because of religious conflicts between the Catholics and Protestants.[48]

Several land claims were made by individuals at the federal land office in Harrison. The first was J.K. Northcutt on August 15, 1879. His homestead entry (No. 4884) was the southeast quarter of the northwest quarter of Section 15, which included the Basin Spring. On the same day, Robert Alexander claimed as his homestead much of the rest of West Mountain and the valley bottom that was becoming the Main Street business district (No. 4885). While those who were coming to the spring for healing had little concern for these details, a dispute over the ownership of the land would weigh heavily on the leadership of Eureka Springs for the next five years.

More Springs Are Discovered

As campers and new residents explored the surrounding hillsides, additional springs were found. Up the holler to the south of the basin, the Conway family settled on the street named for the surveyor Armstrong. The Conways were just one of dozens of Irish immigrant families seeking a new life and choosing to help build this sensational new spa city in the wilderness. David S. Conway was head of the family, a cooper by trade. His wife, Catherine; their son, David J., a carpenter; and their four young daughters, Mary, Catherine, Martha and Rose, lived adjacent to the spring that bears their name.

Wandering the hollows of West Mountain, J. Emmett Harding discovered a seep near a distinctive rock outcropping about midway up the mountain. Digging with picks and shovels, men removed the loose earth from around the seep to reveal that the spring discharged from the base of the giant rock. Harding built his small dwelling near the spring in the summer of 1879 and began the tradition of making photographs of people in front of the spring as souvenirs.

Conway Spring.

Harding Spring.

A naturally flat "bench," as it came to be called, that skirted the contour of the hillside was wide enough for a narrow, precipitous wagon track in front of the spring. Workmen removed all the alluvium from in front of the formation, most likely using it as fill for a building site nearby. The following year, Clark and Hutchings grocery and many new boardinghouses were built, and the Harding Spring Community was rolling. The rate of flow was similar to the basin, and testimonies of cures affected by its use began to circulate, making it second in importance to the primary spring.

The third community to gather around the newly discovered springs was located north of the basin, at the level of the creek bed. Two outpourings with distinctly different properties were called Iron and Sulphur Springs. Lloyd and Evans built a large hotel, the St. Charles. Mr. Evans was not happy that a squatters' village quickly grew around the springs and had to be satisfied that "the whole endeavor was called Evansville."

The fourth community was more of a hilltop settlement than the others, and residents there had access to the springs in the steep gulches on the opposite side of West Mountain, including Johnson, Oil, Moccasin,

Most new arrivals would have passed this way up Main Street to arrive at Basin Spring.

Sycamore, Arsenic and many others. Woodruff's sawmill near what is now Planer Hill and a wagon yard and horse stable near the present Inn of the Ozarks Convention Center were some of the early businesses. D.H. Hopper, upon hearing of the boom in northwest Arkansas, sold his farm in Polk County, Arkansas, and loaded his family into a wagon bound for Eureka Springs. "He stopped to camp in South Eureka, and there he stayed, setting up a grocery business."[49] The settlement later spread eastward along the ridge and became known as New Town.

These four communities soon blended into one and became the four wards of the city. Spring Street was the best way up the mountain, a gradual incline from Main Street to the bench. Soon it was lined on both sides with buildings. Mountain Street went from Main straight up the hill, where it met with the ridge-top route to South Eureka.

A TEN-YEAR-OLD'S VIEW

In the fall of 1879, a young Giles Miller found life in the camp a bit unsettling:[50]

> *Father had fitted out three wagons we had used on the old farm in Kansas, and moved the family and household goods, and what a journey it was. Mortal never came in contact with rougher roads or more*

obstructions. We practically had to cut our way through a wilderness of woods and rocks. I was not yet ten years old, and how strange these hills looked to me. White tents were everywhere apparent, and in the bright sunlight, the contrast with the Autumn leaves and green pines made a sight never to be forgotten. Rude shanties were being constructed by the hundreds—one end of the foundations resting on the hill sides, the other end on pine posts varying in height from three to thirty feet. Time was too precious then to dig for foundations, and besides, the lot "jumper" was abroad and he carried a gun. Possession usually amounts to nine points in the law, but the cautious settler considered possession a quick shanty worth nine hundred and ninety-nine points, or the whole thing. And such streets—the lightning's flash could hardly portray the zig-zags they presented. The fork of a hickory limb was a convenient and almost necessary aid in navigation.

The hundreds of people pouring into the town daily from all points of the compass and from all social classes added to the uniqueness. The cowboy, the dude and the sporting man were here in all their glory, and the "meetings" were many and interesting. I remember that during the period while father was building our house, we occupied a little shanty below the level of Spring street, and I have dug the bullets from its frame work with my jackknife mornings after some of the boys had had "a good time." But along with these were many of the best of people, who came in search of health and a home, and they are still here.

A reporter for the *Arkansas Gazette* wrote that 1,500 lots had been surveyed by December 1879. He estimated a population of three thousand and only five hundred houses that were ready for winter. Boardinghouses and hotels were built and opened to fill the need. The City Hotel, the Eureka House, the Planters' House and the Gilmore House were some of these.

The Southern Hotel soon towered on a rise above the basin. It was built by L.M. Rainey, who had suffered from a number of health conditions and had been an invalid for thirty years before he came to the springs from Springfield, Missouri. He reported problems with his kidneys, rheumatism, torpid liver and dyspepsia. Upon arrival, he stopped taking all the medicines he had been using and began drinking the water. At fifty years of age, he said that he had done more work in that one year than he had in any of the last thirty.[51]

Spring 1880

The first major publicity of the boom of the city in the hills was in February 1880. The story of the boom and claims of healing was covered in a Bentonville newspaper and then spread via a railroad company publication. On Valentine's Day, the city's petition for incorporation was accepted by the county court. Alvah Jackson, Major Cooper, William Nicols and Sine Creeley were photographed in honor of having a fifteen-year reunion at the springs where the men had convalesced during the Civil War under the care of Dr. Jackson.

In his letters, Professor Clarke described Eureka Springs as a destination for throngs of people who entered by way of Berryville one year after Judge Saunders camped there:[52]

> *The springs where my wife was killed have within the last year acquired much fame on account of the curative properties of the water. Rheumatism, scrofula, chronic sore eyes, cancer, gravel and indeed, nearly every kind of chronic disease, are said to be cured by the use of the water of Eureka Springs. The people are wildly excited over the matter. All this Spring the roads have been lined with wagons and other vehicles pressing forward to "Eureka." Where a year ago, there was no town and only a few camps, now there is a city, sprung into existence as if by magic. It is estimated that there are twelve thousand inhabitants in the place.*
>
> *The five or six saw mills convenient to the place are scarcely able to supply the demand for lumber, so rapidly is building going on. The greater part of the buildings are plain box houses, yet there are some fine houses, costing several thousand dollars in their structure. Two papers are published in the place, the* Echo *and the* Herald. *They are scattered pretty well throughout the country.*

Heralding and echoing the glad tidings of the waters that healed, hundreds of these newspapers were soon sent all over the country to relatives and friends of those persons visiting the springs. This publicity helped to bring more and more people, even though travel to Eureka Springs was a real hardship. A stagecoach line began transporting passengers from the train station at Pierce City, Missouri, to the springs for three dollars per person. Called the "Nine-Hour Line," it forded Roaring River nineteen times in one nine-mile stretch. Others took a steamboat up the Arkansas River to Ozark and then came north by stage. This nineteen-hour ride over what is still called the "Pig Trail" (Arkansas Highway 23) was eight dollars per person.[53] Arrivals outnumbered departures by about three to one, with from sixty to one hundred arrivals per day.[54]

The first election of town officers was held on April 6, 1880. E. Rosson was the elected mayor; C.F. Hattenhauer, recorder; and Jasper Hooker, R.R. Pace, George Beavers, W.H. Jones and John Holder, the councilmen. The first note in the official minute book about public grounds was on April 27, 1880. Ordinance No. 10 was passed to prevent trespass on the public grounds (likely referring to squatters building on Basin Spring reservation).

On May 10, 1880, Mayor Rosson made application on behalf of the people of Eureka Springs at the land office in Harrison. He entered all of Section 15, the southern half of Section 10 and a small part of Section 14 as the town site. Unfortunately, it was not that simple. Other claims had been made, and a mineral claim would be filed on July 19, 1880, all of which would have to be sorted out in the courts, a process that would take the next five years. Until the city had legal claim to the town site, it was severely limited in its options for collecting taxes, thus hindering its ability to provide needed services for the growing population.

On May 24, 1880, Jackson and Smith, proprietors of the Mountain House, petitioned the council to allow them to build a stairway up the steep hill behind the spring to their boardinghouse above. Thomas Jackson had sold his bathhouse to John Tibbs, who began a water shipping business from the site.

The lights of campfires still flickered in the evening as people prepared supper, but just one year following Judge Saunders's initial visit, it was an entirely different scene. On May 25, 1880, Alvah Jackson passed away at his home on the Kings. Saunders would meet his eternal reward in 1881, but the ball was rolling and was not about to stop.

Chapter 8

A TOWN OF FIFTEEN THOUSAND

During the chaotic frenzy of the early town, miners sought to develop mineral claims in the area around the springs. Sinking shafts frequently over and near the springs, the miners struck fear in the hearts of the townspeople and health seekers. Finally, while sinking a shaft above the basin, they struck water.

> *And the townspeople feared that the water of the Basin Spring was threatened. An indignation meeting of the populace was hurriedly called. The unanimous feeling of those present was that the springs be protected at all costs and by any means. A motion to that effect was passed and a committee was named to call on the miners and demand that their digging cease, while other citizens went about filling up the holes already dug. Thus ended, for the time, the mining activity in Eureka Springs.[55]*

Some of the first doctors to arrive were Dr. J.O. Drucker, Dr. William Johnston, Dr. William Reese and Dr. Pearl Hale Tatman. Dr. Johnston said:

> *The action of our waters in the cure of disease is well marked, and although opinions may be divided as to how they cure, all are agreed that they cure. Some may say that there is no virtue in medicinal waters and the cures are due to other causes. Then, we say, show us what the causes are.[56]*

Professor L.J. Kalklosch was a teacher in the Normal School at Harrison, forty-five miles east of Eureka Springs. He had been hearing from visitors who had come to see for themselves, as well reading about it in his local papers. They wondered at the cause of the cures. Some supposed it was imagination;

A growing town, 1881. The dark structure in the center is the Perry House under construction. The pine grove is the Basin Spring Reservation.

others thought it was "the pure air and change of surroundings." It didn't matter to many what was the cause, "but a decided and incontrovertible truth was established: People did receive benefits and cures. This was enough for the afflicted to know; they cared nothing about the 'how' or 'why' it cured."

In May 1880, Kalklosch was forced to retire after suffering with "a very severe attack of typho-malarial fever." He decided to find out for himself whether these springs worked and described his first impressions:

After having traveled a seeming great distance over the hills and through the dense forests, the driver informed us that we were on the "Eureka Mountain." Here a splendid mountain breeze saluted us, and the pine trees were waving as if in welcome to those traveling beneath their foliage.

The smooth road, the bracing atmosphere, and the vast scenery of the northern Arkansas hills and forests, caused us to forget that we were approaching the new Eldorado until the silence of the forest, was broken by the bustle of the busy throng below. We had indeed reached the summit of the mountain just over the city. The thought of having traveled for miles through a wilderness region, and all of a sudden emerging in full view of a city of 10,000 or 12,000 souls, clamoring on the hill-sides and in the gulches, naturally filled us with admiration.

People coming into the city on their first approach dared not stop to think. In spite of all that had been said, and the cures that had been effected, if a person stopped, looked over the scene, saw the hundreds of little houses going up, and the (so called) streets (paths) lined with people carrying pails and kegs of every description, going to the springs for water—the old, the young, the lame, the blind, the fat, the lean, the dyspeptic, and the dropsical—in short, people of all ages and diseases, all seemingly expecting to be made youthful and whole—the feeling, and frequently the expression: "What nonsense!" would force its way, wholly involuntary on his part.

After he took "a course" of spring water, he stayed in the fledgling town, writing a history called *The Healing Fountain*, published a year later, in 1881. He described finding two thousand houses and only three streets that could be considered thoroughfares: Main, Spring and Mountain. The streets were wide enough that only when wagons and their teams went in the same direction could they travel safely. When they met, one would have to back up "at times several rods" (one rod equals five and a half yards) to allow passage.

Stories of Healing

Jennie Cowen also had remarkable results. The twenty-year-old had been blind for seven years following an illness. She had been using the waters of Basin Spring for several months and then changed to Harding Spring. On August 22, 1880, she exclaimed, "I can see!" Her sight was restored. She later wrote to Professor Kalklosch: "I will say that my faith in the Spring is unbounded." She signed off "with a pleasant recollection of the kind agreeable people of your Mountain City, and a grateful heart for my restored sight."

W.T. Dickens had been a helpless invalid when he came in 1879, severely afflicted with rheumatism. When he returned home at Christmas, his family noticed that he was much improved. In February 1880, his son John and some friends wanted to see this wonderful fountain of youth. They drove up Main Street to Gadd Spring and wondered if they could get their team and empty hack up Mountain Street. When they saw one of the lumber wagons go up with a team of little mules, they gave it a try. They found John's father

Jennie Cowen at the basin, 1880.

camped on Center Street. John decided to stay in Eureka Springs and got a job working nights filling barrels of water for the Basin Spring Water Company. His father was entirely cured and lived to be an old man.[57]

Ague, which came to be called malaria, had long been a kind of rite of passage for pioneers locating to the Arkansas lowlands. Hot August nights would find them huddled around roaring fires, shaking violently with an internal chill alternating with a raging fever. Many found relief for this condition at the springs. Dr. J.H. Smithers arrived in Eureka in August 1881. He had not been able to eat or sleep for three weeks. He waited in a long line until he could get to the spring, where he dipped out a pail full of water. Then he went over to a shade tree and drank it all. He waited his turn again and got another bucketful, which he carried to his room at the Kansas House, where he drank it all that night. In the morning, he could eat a hearty breakfast and continued to improve. After three weeks of using the waters, he was cured.

The line between subsistence and too-weary-to-go-on was crossed for the Fortners of Taney County when their son Amon developed polio. Jacob Fortner and his children had suffered chills and fever each fall, and his wife, Malissia, "was in poor health, losing several babies prematurely." Seeking healing and a chance to make a living, they came to the springs in 1881, arriving with little more than the clothes on their backs. Jacob found a job at Mrs. Massman's lumberyard paying $0.50 per day, and Powell Clayton allowed them to live in various squatters' shacks awaiting sale. The Fortners bought three lots for $100.00, paying $5.00 down and $2.00 per month. It proved to be more than they could afford.[58] Amon went on to be a prolific writer.

After visiting, Amos Lundy returned home to Indiana and brought his wife and family to the springs in 1882. He took a lot, had it surveyed and began to improve it. He found a trickle of water, traced it and discovered what came to be called Crescent Spring. His wife and child were soon cured, and the family settled down to make a life in the new town.

Joseph Perry grew up in a hotel family in New Jersey. By the time he was nineteen, he had his own hotel. He made his way west to the frontier, building hotels along the way. He knew many of the legendary figures of the Wild West at Fort Hays and Kit Carson and other towns along the railroad as tracks were laid across the plains. By the time he was thirty-eight, his health was in decline. He arrived among the first health seekers in 1879. After regaining his health, he resolved not to leave the life-giving fountain and built the beautiful Perry House next to Basin Spring. He made Basin Spring water available in every room of his hotel.

During the 1881–82 period, a weekly meeting of invalids was held at the Elk Street ME Church, "and the cures recited in these assemblages were many and miraculous." The diseases by which they were afflicted included cancer, asthma, scrofula, sore eyes, spinal disease, dyspepsia, paralysis, hemorrhoids, female troubles, etc.[59] The purpose of the Invalids' Association was to provide information about cures, as well as hotels, boardinghouses and other matters of interest to visitors. In 1884, it was meeting twice monthly. "The happy results from the use of these 'magic' waters were very encouraging to invalids who had more recently arrived at the Springs, and especially if the disease cured was similar to their own."[60]

First Impressions

Railroad tracks had been laid to a new town close to the Missouri-Arkansas border. Named for Joseph Seligman, a New York banker and financier of the Frisco, Seligman was just twenty miles from Eureka Springs. Soon, a road was hacked out along Butler Creek to the White River and then up Leatherwood Creek, coming into the north end of Main Street. This was a minor challenge for the wagoners and stage coachmen, who were used to the tough routes from Pierce City and Ozark.

On August 16, 1881, the city was awarded the status of city of the second class, and on October 26, it became a city of the first class. With five thousand legal residents, Eureka Springs was the fourth-largest city in Arkansas.[61]

According to Kalklosch, around that time the stage route from Seligman into town "has been very objectionable to many invalids, because of the roughness of the road." He went on to say that the road was being improved, and a better class of stagecoaches would be forthcoming.

A reporter for the *New York Daily Graphic* traveled this route in May 1882:[62]

Situated among the mountains, or great hills, of northwestern Arkansas, the only convenient and comfortable way of approach is via St. Louis, over the St. Louis and San Francisco Railway, to Seligman, for where a stage ride of eighteen or twenty miles brings the traveler to the Mecca of that region. From Seligman to Eureka Springs is a wild, sparsely inhabited, mountainous district, and at places the scenery becomes fascinating. From the station the stage pitches at once into a gulch between the mountains and toils on, now hugging the mountain side, now following some stream, and at rare intervals gaining the mountaintop. Six or more miles on the way the Missouri and Arkansas line is passed, where two magnificent springs, one on either side of the line mark the State boundary. Half way along, White River, a mountain stream famous for fish and giving a name to the mountains, is crossed. Fortunately, and owing to the enterprise of Colonel Nisbet, of Mississippi, the crossing is now made on a substantial bridge, while formerly a ferry, consuming at certain seasons an hour's time, has been the only means of transfer. Two miles from White River, Leatherwood Creek, a typical mountain stream, sullen and moody, now a gentle brook flashing merrily in the sunbeams, and now a perfect torrent, is met, and following its winding course the city is finally reached. The roads are rough; the heavy Concord coaches have been dragged over boulders and rocks and through mud and deep ruts at a plodding rate until every bone aches, and you are glad when the city is sighted. But your weariness is soon dispelled, for if the novelty of the ride and quiet beauty of the scenery have not compensated for the tediousness of the journey, the scene as you catch the first glimpse of the city will balance the account.

About his first impression, he had this to say:

The counterpart cannot be found in all America. The mountains are 600 to 1,000 feet high. Six or more gulches meet forming the city's site, and on the sides of the various mountains, with scarcely a foot of level ground, the city has been built. The houses rise tier above tier, and cling to the mountainside like a frightened monkey to a bareback horse, each structure being in immediate peril of going roof first into the gulch below. The streets, at places eighty feet apart, are fully half that distance above each other, they mount one above the other like giant steps; the buildings, four stories in front, are one storied in the rear, or vice versa. Building lots for structures of any importance are gained only by blasting, and so rapidly is this being pushed that each arrival may well imagine the constant sound of blasting to be so many salutes fired in his honor. The entire city, with the exception of one building, is built of pine. With less than half a dozen exceptions the structures are mere shanties, hardly worthy of the name houses, although perhaps a few hotels and larger boarding houses should be excepted. But in June, 1879, where now stands Eureka Springs, with 12,000 to 15,000 inhabitants, the primeval quiet had scarcely been disturbed.

The following five photographs were featured in a full-page spread in the *Daily Graphic*. They were turned into engravings for the purpose of publishing.

Tank at Basin Spring, 1882.

Arsenic Spring, 1882.
Courtesy Arkansas Historical Commission.

Southern Hotel reveals the Black Dog statue to the left of the stairway (not shown in illustration).

Dairy Spring, 1882.

Shelter near Johnson Spring, 1882.

Chapter 9

IMPROVEMENTS

B asin Spring had been the central focal point of the community since the beginning. Some of the earliest improvements around the spring were due to the heavy traffic of health seekers making their pilgrimages to take the waters. "Wastewater," as the runoff was called, was collected and used in the first bathhouse, as well as in others to follow.

Eureka Springs Water Company shipped Basin Spring water. A system of pipes ran down the hill from a source above the basin so that barrels could be filled. The water shippers had to work at night due to the volume of health seekers at the spring.

The steep hillside below the basin was transformed into Basin Spring Avenue. In October 1881, city government granted J.A. Newman the right to erect an elevator from near the basin to the Southern Hotel. It may have been difficult for many invalids to walk up and down a flight of seventy-five steps, so a tower and lift with a walkway more than thirty feet high was constructed. By midsummer, the right was repealed, and the elevator had to be removed.

THE RAILROAD COMES TO TOWN

The Eureka Springs Railway Company was chartered on June 26, 1880, with former Arkansas governor Powell Clayton as president. Before the war, Powell Clayton had been a surveyor and then city engineer in Leavenworth, Kansas. Civil engineering was just becoming a profession in the Victorian era. His time in Kansas had given him a vision of what a frontier town could be, and he employed his organizational skills in several major projects in Eureka Springs.

Above: Filling barrels and "taking the waters" at Basin Spring.

Right: Basin Spring Avenue descends to Main Street from the spring under the "Balm of Life" sign, winter 1881–82.

A "Balm of Life"
sign advertising John
Tibbs's Eureka Water
Condensing Company.

The bustling downtown
area directly opposite
Basin Spring, 1882.

Bringing the railroad from Seligman to town was a high-priced endeavor. Capitalized at $1.5 million, or $25,000 per mile, it was the most expensive length of track in the United States.[63] Opened on February 1, 1883, Eureka Spring Railroad brought prosperity to the town as a health spa, as well as a commercial center. The depot was at the edge of town, just outside the disputed town site area.

TOWN SITE QUESTION

Ownership of property in Eureka Springs was a question until 1885. As reported in 1882, improvements were taking place to accommodate the townspeople and visitors:

> *With the title to the land unsettled, and with no corporate existence, the city's affairs had been in a tangle. After various shifts had been adopted, one Mayor impeached, and other officers found inefficient, if not dishonest, Captain John Carroll, a veteran six-footer and native of Arkansas, was elected Mayor in the spring of 1881. Under his efficient administration chaos has been reduced to order, scrip has been issued, and the main thoroughfares put into better condition. Sanitary affairs have been attended to, and while much must yet be done to place the city's condition upon a right basis, everything is orderly, and the streets, although very narrow, are improved and passable.[64]*

In February 1881, Mayor John Carroll had applied for entry as a town site at the land office in Harrison but was refused on the grounds that proceedings were in process to determine the character of the land in question. He and Captain Ingraham went to Washington, D.C., to represent the city before the General Land Commission. An initial decision that went against the farmers and allowed the mineral and township claims was later overturned by the secretary of the interior. In late 1882, testimony was taken establishing the existence of a community before either the farmers or the miners arrived. Finally, in July 1883, Commissioner McFarland decided in favor of city authorities, but the case was appealed by the agricultural claimants.

Powell Clayton and the Eureka Springs Improvement Company (ESIC) instituted proceedings to test the legality of the township title in federal district court in 1884. Townspeople wanted to resolve the issue.

The city council asked citizens to seek a solution. At an initial meeting chaired by Joe Ivey, a proposition from ESIC was not approved. Another meeting, with John Carroll presiding, went on for twelve hours until a settlement was reached at four o'clock in the morning. The compromise was reflected in the official decree made by the United States District Court on April 6, 1885.

Leaseholders in the disputed area would be given deeds. In the contested portion of Section 15, where most of the springs were located, they were given deeds signed by Mayor Archimedes Davis, as well as Powell Clayton, president of the Improvement Company, and John Carroll, representing the citizens' interests. The spring reservations were to belong to the city, and churches were to receive lots without compensation.

"All property unclaimed within a specified period would revert without compensation to the Improvement Company. A commission representing all interests was provided for which was to have jurisdiction in the widening of streets, abatement of nuisances and removal of unoccupied houses. The company was granted the right to operate street car lines, also gas and water pipe lines, for a period of fifty years."[65]

Reservations for springs were officially recorded in ordinances defining their metes and bounds on February 15, 1886. These included Little Eureka, Cave and Maxwell, Cold, Iron, Laundry, Harding, East Mountain, Table Rock (Calef), Oak (Grotto) or Sheffield and Sweet or Spout Spring Reservations.[66] Dr. Johnston's 1884 guidebook, *The Eureka Springs, Arkansas*, gives the number of springs within the city as forty-two.

FIRE AND WATER

There had been no major fires in the first five years of the City of Healing Waters. Henry Marshall had been appointed fire warden when that position was established in May 1880. A bucket brigade had sufficed until the night of November 3, 1883. Arson was considered as the cause, as the fire began in a business at the base of Mountain Street. Wooden shacks caught one another on fire with such rapidity that the bucket-toting volunteers could not make a dent in the blaze. Up Mountain and Eureka Streets, a five-acre area, seventy-five homes and commercial buildings were consumed. A second fire in 1888 burned every commercial building on Spring Street, from Hancock House near Sweet Spring to Perry House next to Basin Spring.

The first Flatiron Building stands to the left of the devastation of the 1888 Spring Street fire.

The people petitioned for the development of an adequate water system. Before the waterworks were completed, two more fires destroyed the Perry House, Grand Central Hotel and the establishments on South Main to Calef Spring, including the Hughes House and the Western Hotel.

Sycamore Spring had the highest flow by far of all the springs in the area. Located in the gulch opposite South Town near Arsenic Spring, the two springs discharged nearly sixty thousand gallons per day, whereas Basin and Crescent each flowed at eleven thousand gallons per day.[67] Fourteen additional springs named for trees were located in the hollow: Blackgum, Elm, Post Oak, Walnut, Red Oak, Catalpa, Blackhaw, Service Tree, Hickory, Red Cedar, Dog Wood, Redbud, White Ash and Mulberry. In addition to these, Little Magnetic and Saucer Spring contributed to what became the City Reservoir, now Black Bass Lake.

Above: A cut stone dam enclosed the City Reservoir, 1895.

Left: The Stand Pipe, circa 1895, is still in service today adjacent to Inn of the Ozarks.

Panorama with the standpipe at center horizon, from the observation deck atop the Crescent Hotel, circa 1900. This view shows reforestation two decades after the initial building boom.

More than a decade earlier, in November 1881, some ingenious citizens of South Eureka had installed a force-pump appliance to supply the community with water from Arsenic Spring.[68] Professor L.J. Kalklosch called it "a kind of 'water telegraph,' to convey the water from the spring to the top of the hill." A system of steam pumps brought the water up from the dam site to an iron standpipe atop West Mountain.

On April 5, 1895, the water system began operation, and the Municipal Fire Department was soon ready to respond with three hose companies stationed in different parts of the city. A quick response to an alarm of fire was now possible.

Consumers could pay by a set annual fee or have a water meter installed and pay at a graduated rate. Preferring spring water to "pond water," a majority of the people continued to carry water from the springs for drinking and used city water for other purposes.

Sweet Spring

A spring in the deep ravine between Center Street and Harding Spring was often a gathering place for baptisms. It was then called Spout Spring.

Also known as Sweet or Sweetwater Spring, the stream of water was traced back to its source in the limestone bluff uphill from where it was originally found. Instead of removing all the alluvial fill in front of the

Health seekers gather at the site of the original Sweet Spring, circa 1882.

A walking bridge over the ravine, looking toward Sweet Spring. The original site of Sweet Spring is at the lower left.

Stonework at Sweet Spring, 1895.

spring, a circular enclosure was built around the outlet, and the road then called Rice Street remained in front of the spring.

This was an important spring for business purposes; a laundry and a bathhouse used the water. William, James and John Waldrip did the stone work in 1885, and wood sidewalks were built around that time.

THE CRESCENT

The Crescent Hotel, built by the Eureka Springs Improvement Company and the Frisco Railroad, was opened to the public on May 10, 1886, under the management of G.W. Kittelle. Limestone from the quarries on the White River was precisely cut and fit in place under the direction of a group of masons brought in from Ireland. The five-story hotel was designed by architect Isaac Taylor.[69] Water from Crescent and Congress Springs was pumped up from their locations on the hillside below. The grand hotel symbolized a new era of luxury, convenience and service for Eureka Springs as a resort catering to vacationers and health seekers—the "carriage set." Nellie Mills wrote about a visit to the Crescent Hotel: "The party entered the rotunda and drank Basin, Dairy, or Sweet

Above: Original pavilion at Crescent Spring.

Left: Gazebo at Crescent Spring, circa 1886.

Spring water from a tank where it is labeled like a soda fountain." Guests were also furnished in their rooms, morning and night, with water from any spring desired.

WATER AND SANITATION

The city could not collect taxes on personal property until the town site dispute was settled, so finances for services were slim to none. Even so, citizens called for regulations concerning sanitary conditions such as water supply, sewers and sewage disposal. A board of health was appointed as early as the fall of 1880.

Basin Spring was visited by hundreds of health seekers each day, many drinking quarts of fresh water. The nearby businesses felt the pressure of the traffic and needed improved sanitary facilities. On April 21, 1882, I.A. Numan asked for permission from the city to "erect a sewer to conduct slops from the Southern hotel in the sewer near Basin Springs."[70] A few days later, a statement from the local board of health was presented to the council recommending that permission be granted to Numan and Joseph Perry to run a sewer from the Southern and Perry House connecting to the sewer near Basin Spring.

The 1878 Memphis epidemic had focused the nation's attention on new standards of sanitation. A National Board of Health was created in March 1879, and it conducted an in-depth survey. It chose George E. Waring's system in which sewage waste was separated from storm-water runoff and this reduced the size of pipes needed to carry septic sewage. In 1886, the Waring system was used by the Crescent Hotel, carrying effluent one and a half miles to Leatherwood Creek.[71]

The city sewage disposal system, begun in 1890, was completed in 1895. City engineer John W. Riley designed a network and hired local workmen to lay the pipes and mains within the corporate limits. Private lines from homes and businesses were connected to this system. Dumping into the stream was thought to be an improvement over cesspools, cesspits or fields of decaying organic matter, which produced miasmas that were thought to cause disease. According to Waring, "The whole household drainage of a town should be carried immediately into a river by cleanly flushed sewers."

The sewer system flowed into the creek for a decade before a septic tank and plant were built. Sanitary reform had helped end a long series of epidemics in Memphis and other cities. Waring's innovations in sewerage continued to be used by city planners to remove the "byproducts of urbanization."

Wastewater had formerly referred to water discharged at a spring that was not immediately contained and used. This type of wastewater was regulated by the city as a cherished commodity to be used freely by all people and was also tapped by commercial enterprises, including shippers, hotels, laundries and bathhouses. Wastewater actually referring to sewage would mark an important shift in the consciousness of Eurekans.

In the 1880s and 1890s, German and French scientists, including Robert Koch and Louis Pasteur, identified the microscopic organisms responsible for diseases such as anthrax, tuberculosis and cholera. Soon, sanitary reform would shift to the filtration and chlorination of these microbes.

BASIN PARK

The basin remained the "center" of town, and after a decade of heavy traffic, it must have been showing signs of wear. Originally there was an additional basin down from the famed one:

> *Below this basin twelve feet there was originally another basin in the rock, a portion of which had been destroyed previous to the discovery of the springs. This basin had apparently been five feet in length and ten to twelve inches in depth. The width could not be ascertained, as it was parallel to the gulch, and had probably been destroyed by one of the huge rocks that had fallen from the ledge above. When the present improvements were being made in the vicinity of the spring, the gulch was converted into a culvert to carry the surplus water from the spring, and it became necessary to blast the rocks.* [72]

In 1890, the Eureka Springs Board of Public Affairs created a formal setting for Basin Spring. Limestone walls around a semicircular park, the promenade was above the spring with a wishing well to look down at the basin a dozen feet below. Faucets for filling cups and containers were available at both a round decorative fountain and a square pedestal upon which an art nouveau fairy sat. The first fountain sprayed upward from the raised hands of a child, possibly an allusion to the Fountain of Youth.

According to the editor of the *Eureka Springs Medical Journal,* "The recent improvement at the Basin Spring reflect credit on the authorities as well as the general cleaning they have given the city. An old-time visitor remarked this morning that he had never seen the town so clean and in such good

Above: Basin Spring improvements, early 1890s.

Right: A next stage of improvements included a second tier and walkway around the semicircle. Electric lines indicate a late 1890s date.

order."[73] Cleanliness was ever more important to the doctors of this era as germs were just beginning to be understood: "Everything now indicates that we are to have a good season. The sanitary condition was never so good, and will be kept to the mark, and the streets and sidewalks as well as the improvements about the springs altogether will make a visit here for the invalid or pleasure seeker better than ever before."

SANITARIUM LAKE

Dr. Charles E. Davis, a Chicago physician, brought his wife to the springs for a cure. They built a home named for their daughter, Crystal. The Crystal Terrace stood on West Mountain; later, Dr. Davis suggested to Powell Clayton the top of the mountain as the location for his fine hotel.

In 1890, Davis and his financial backers, Ralph E. Brownell, Davitt D. Chidester and Dr. M.R. Regan, established the Eureka Sanitarium Company. Brownell's company later constructed the water tower still standing on West Mountain.

Marble Arch Bridge, 1893.

Facilities about three miles south of town provided an 1,800-acre park for outdoor recreation. A small spring-fed lake called Mountain Lake was enlarged and renamed Sanitarium Lake. Swimming and boating, as well as horseback riding on well-groomed trails around the lake, were promoted. Beautiful arched bridges, now on the National Register of Historic Places, spanned two of the ravines on the Lake Road.

The trend in curative science was toward combining healthful pleasure with the best medical skill. Dr. Davis brought in Dr. William B. Sprague from Battle Creek, Michigan, to manage Sanitarium Medical Services. At their office in town, they offered medical treatments as stated in an 1897 brochure:[74]

> *The marvelous and undeniable power of our waters, climate and altitude in reaching chronic, obscure and complicated diseases of all kinds had been well attested by the thousands of cures effected here by these natural conditions alone…Intelligent observers both in and out of the medical profession have long been impressed with the importance of proper hygienic care and instruction in the use of these natural advantages, more especially in the matter of drinking and bathing, in connection with proper exercise, diet and medicine when needed…*
>
> *Our facilities enable us to give expert electrical treatment (including the sinusoidal current) and massage, in all their forms…We also give the radiant bath, which has proven so efficient an improvement upon the Turkish and Russian baths; also, in connection with our treatment, all forms of tub baths—needle, sitz, leg, etc., with or without massage, as indicated.*

After his wife's death in 1920, Dr. Davis retired and sold the sanitarium grounds and lake to Richard R. Thompson, then president of Crescent College. He renamed it Lake Lucerne, built a lodge, cabins, dance pavilion and golf course, and the resort remained popular through the 1960s.

Chapter 10

THE BOULEVARD

The streetcar made its way up Hillside Avenue from the train depot, joining with the main line in front of Crescent Spring. To the left, Spring Street led through the business district to the Basin Spring Park. To the right was the Boulevard, a relatively wide, level street that followed the contour of the mountain to the Summer Assembly grounds.

Crescent Spring, named for a large crescent-shaped ledge of rocks, was revered for its healing waters. Retaining walls of Beaver limestone lined the sidewalk. A scenic public walking trail began at a stone stairway to the side of the spring. Wooden benches and gas streetlamps were in place by 1886, when the Presbyterian church across the Boulevard from the spring was constructed. Next to the church was Crescent Cottage, the Governor Powell Clayton family home.

Two doors down on the same side was Chautauqua House, facing Pence House, both fine hotels. Nellie Mills described the scene: "They walked on, passing high stone walls that had been built to make level lawns, passing also some of the richest and most beautiful residences in the town." She noted that the street was not paved but well graded. "On the right, as they passed, were many houses, the second stories of which were on a level with the street while on the left the houses were high above the street."

Other beautiful homes lined the Boulevard, such as the Bridgeford Cottage in the Queen Anne style. Cozy Corner was the home of Drs. Pearl and A.E. Tatman. The Rosalie was originally the home of J.W. Hill, the livery owner who was instrumental in bringing the first telephone to town. Much of the gingerbread ornamentation was the handiwork of W.O. Perkins at his mill on Center Street.[75]

Where the Boulevard begins.

Sightseers from the Chatauqua House onboard Talley Ho, circa 1895.

Family and guests at Pence House on the Boulevard, circa 1890.

The street turned westward into Dairy Hollow as the houses were left behind. Nellie Mills continued, "On one side trees and bluffs arose, on the other trees and bluffs fell away to the gulch which ascends gradually…Only one object of interest stopped them. This was the Grotto spring which they found a delightfully cool place for a hot June day."

The circular opening at the cave entrance was the work of skilled stone masons in 1885. A carved plaque stating "Esto Perpetua" set into stone the sentiments that the healing waters would flow perpetually from this site. Once known as Twin Springs, it supplied the waterworks at the train depot at the base of the hollow.[76]

Continuing farther on the Boulevard one came to Dairy Spring, named for the dairy operated by the Sheffield family. In the early days, health seekers would walk over the mountain from the basin or Harding to the valley on the other side to enjoy a cool drink. In 1881, a survey of the area made by John E. Perrin was added to the plat map of the town site. In August of that year, a tank was erected at the spring. A rustic shed-roofed structure was placed over the spring that was later replaced by a Swiss chalet–style cover with bench seating.

The Grotto Spring, a favorite of visitors and photographers.

The Interstate Normal Summer Assembly grounds were located at Dairy Spring from 1891 to 1906. A course of lectures and Chautauqua programs were offered to entertain visitors. A spring-fed natatorium for swimming and croquet and tennis courts were also on site. Nellie Mills attended the first session designed to train teachers.

Later, she wrote about the Summer Auditorium in her novel, *A Story of the Ozarks*:

> *A rustic entrance leads into the grounds. A stone's throw from this entrance is the structure that gives the place its name.*
>
> *It is a self-supporting, circular building. At the lower side—that is, the side facing an arm of the gulch—a stage has been placed. Then circling the rest of the perimeter are the rows of inclined seats. On the side nearest the entrance this amphitheater rests upon the ground, while at either end it is supported by masonry.*
>
> *They descended the central aisle of the amphitheater to the parquet which is also supplied with benches.*
>
> *At one side the water from the Dairy Springs has been conducted through pipes to a faucet. They drank freely of the cold sparkling water.*
>
> *Crossing to the right of the stage they found a long flight of steps descending, which led them into the dressing rooms under the stage.*

The entrance to the Summer Auditorium and Assembly Grounds, early 1890s.

The Summer Auditorium and Assembly Grounds, established 1891, now Harmon Park.

Ascending again they climbed the outer aisle which rested upon the stone walls the upper edge being something like twenty feet from the ground.

The covered open-air theater was designed and built by W.O. Perkins to seat 3,500 people. After 1906, Perkins converted the theater into a skating rink. The streetcar barn was also located nearby.[77]

VICTORIAN VERSE

Florence Hammersley expressed her pleasure in the landscape in a charming Victorian-era poem written around 1900:

There's ever a touch of fragrance
  By the winds caressingly flung
That blends with the plaintive murmur
  By the pine trees ceaselessly sung;
But after a shower falleth
  How it makes one's pulses thrill
To catch the scent of rain-swept pines
  That crown Eureka's hills!

There the purple hush of the twilight
  Alone brings a sense of rest,
After the heat and glamour of day
  Has drifted into the west;
E'en the moonlit nights of Eureka
  Have a glory all their own—
A sort of silvery symphony,
  With pines for an undertone.

As long as memory lasteth
  I shall count 'mid life's sweetest things
The moonlit nights, the scent of pines,
  The hills of Eureka Springs;
Where the purple twilight enfoldeth
  The day with peaceful calm,
And the pine trees lulleth the tired soul
As the strains of an evening psalm.

Chapter 11

THE TURN OF THE CENTURY

I n his *Points* magazine in 1900, editor Giles Miller recalled his arrival as a child in the earliest days of Eureka Springs. He wanted others to remember the wonderful cures and natural beauty surrounding the resort. He had watched as the native pine structures, so closely packed, housed some twenty-two thousand people in 1881. The old Eureka had faded, consumed by fires and now replaced by substantial business blocks of stone.

According to Professor L.J. Kalklosch, in the first few years, "every man that could use a hand-saw was a carpenter, and many who had possibly only read a patent medicine almanac were doctors." By the 1890s, the medical profession was making great changes. Robert Koch, a German physician, published his experimental steps known as Koch's postulates, which became the rules for identifying the specific pathogen that caused a particular disease.

The *Eureka Springs Medical Journal* informed doctors about ongoing research such as Eberth's discovery of a type of bacilli found in a typhoid survivor.[78] An understanding of "Typhoid Mary," a carrier who spread the disease without showing symptoms herself, was more than a decade in the future. Other articles included practices for treating Bright's disease or gonorrhea.

In May 1893, Dr. Ellis wrote a long letter to the editor stating some of the merits of homeopathy. Ellis, a homeopathic doctor, was staff physician at the Crescent Hotel. He argued that the discipline was still going strong, with ten thousand homeopathic physicians in the United States, twenty colleges, fifty journals and four national societies. The *Medical Journal* editor, Dr. Reece, countered, "Yes it is cheap, no question about that, and it ought to be cheap considering its intrinsic value."

In 1893, the *Medical Journal* included a warning to physicians:

> *Physicians in sending patients to watering places should caution them against that very accommodating and insinuating class of people politely called drummers, but are in reality a species of the bunco-steerers who infest all such places and whose business it is to run them into a hotel, then to a doctor, then to the bath house and even a drug store, but never once tells his victim that he is being handsomely paid for such services and that the take-off is necessarily added to the bill or else the person paying gets inferior service and pays the highest price.*

In 1891, the Arkansas legislature adopted Act 22, a bill empowering county medical boards to revoke the license of physicians found guilty of "unprofessional conduct," including "moral turpitude, habitual drunkenness, false advertising, using drummers, or participation in abortions."[79]

The Arkansas Association of Pharmacists, founded in 1882, worked to reform medical and drug laws. In 1906, Congress passed a Pure Food and Drug Act with the support of President Theodore Roosevelt. With the national feeling leaning toward regulatory action, the Arkansas legislature passed several bills to deal with patent medicines. In the mid-nineteenth century, many powerful remedies were sold. Alcohol fortified with morphine, opium or cocaine was claimed to cure or prevent about any ailment imaginable. By the turn of the century, facilities to treat patients with addictions to alcohol and narcotics found their home in Eureka Springs.

MAGNETIC HOLLOW

Magnetic Spring was claimed to magnetize any metal object. A wooden pavilion was built over the spring where the flow poured from the hillside through a man-made channel. The Tourist Social Hour Club met at the spring regularly from 1885 to 1935 to share its concerns about entertaining tourists.

In Nellie Mills's novel, her protagonists rode horses down Hillside from the Boulevard to the train depot and then went south on Main Street until they arrived at Magnetic Hollow to the left. The first spring they visited was Magnetic. The water was not as refreshingly cold as other springs in town because it was exposed to the sun. "But it is very clear and sparkling and is said to be as pure as distilled dew."

The Magnetic Spring.

Bell Spring postcard view.

About half a mile from the spring, they came upon a fence:

Milton descended to open and close the gate and did not remount, but led his horse. At one place he led them aside from the path, ascended the hill a short distance to let them see the "Little Bell."

A small stream of water escapes through a crevice in the low bluff. A larger volume of water within the rock seems to be falling, the tinkling sound issuing from within the rock, giving the spring its name.

After leaving the Little Bell, Milton walked quietly on. He wished them to see the Mystic without having it pointed out.

A cry from Margaret testified to her delight.

"This is the grandest of all. How high is that bluff? How can it stand? Won't it fall?"

Mrs. Patterson laughed. "I suppose it has stood there for ages. It will hardly fall today, just because we are here and see it for the first time."

The young people climbed the rocky hillside to more fully explore the site:

Margaret had climbed upon the little shelf, which rested upon the ground on either side of the ravine, the sides of which were far rockier than below the falls, but affording excellent footing, and very easily climbed.

Mystic Spring.

Mystic Spring and bluffs.

Postcard view of Maxfield Barber, age 102, at Magnetic Spring pavilion.

"See how soft this rock is," she said, crumbling it off with her hand. "That's why it has worn so much faster at the bottom. It seems hard higher up. See how straight the strata and how loose some of the layers seem. See up there is a slab six inches thick that looks ready to fall. How does it keep from upsetting. It must be well-balanced in the mountain behind."

"See here," said Milton. "There is a break, and these two bluffs do not seem to have a common origin. The middle ledge is gray. This has a reddish tinge."

MAGNETIC HOTEL AND SANITARIUM

Magnetic Spring and the land around it, known as the Magnetic Forty, came into the possession of Powell Clayton after the court decision of 1885. When Clayton was made ambassador to Mexico in 1899, he and his family left Eureka Springs. The use of Magnetic Spring water was apparently granted to Dr. Reed, of Texas, who had it piped to his new sanitarium across from the hollow on Depot Grade, now Hillside Avenue.

Dr. Reed announced his plan in *Points* magazine in 1900:[80]

I expect to make Eureka Springs my permanent home. When I was here last year my health became much improved, but when I returned to the

Magnetic Spring Sanitarium on Hillside Avenue.

malarial district it declined almost as rapidly. I sold out to my partner, and took hold of this enterprise, resolving to place my interests where I can enjoy health. Nearly all the Magnetic forty acre tract is now in my possession, and I shall keep it as a park, leaving everything clear above the spring, so that its water cannot possibly become interfered with in any way. If nothing interferes, I expect to have the building ready for business by June 1st, and it is my purpose ultimately, to build a row of tenant cottages below the spring.

The sanitarium hotel was a beautiful three-story structure with a basement. On July 18, 1900, the grand opening of Magnetic College and Sanitarium was held. Magnetic Spring water soon had the reputation for curing addictions to alcohol and powerful narcotics that were standard ingredients of the patent medicines of the day. Opium, morphine, laudanum, heroin and cocaine were used in common remedies for soothing teething or colicky babies and lozenges to treat children or adults with strong coughs.

An advertisement for the sanitarium appeared in a 1904 *Daily Times-Echo* featuring Dr. C.A. Reed claiming: "LIQUOR HABIT Cured in one week, MORPHINE HABIT Cured in 15 days. Patients Are Allowed Perfect Liberty at all Times."

According to a 1905 article:

The sanitarium company owns the Magnetic Springs, the waters of which are piped directly into the sanitarium for use, and the virtues of which, combined with the remedies employed, have given the institution such a wonderful reputation for success. Thousands of persons who were addicted to some form of drug slavery or to the vise of drunkenness have been cured here since this sanitarium has been opened, and its management proudly boasts that it has never failed to cure a case, no matter how long standing or apparently desperate. The cures are effected rapidly, and at no time during the treatment are the patients debarred from perfect liberty of action. Hypodermics are never used, neither does sickness or physical collapse result from the treatment. A competent staff of physicians is always on duty at the sanitarium to attend to the treatment of the patients and look out for their welfare.

Several managers and doctors were associated with the facility from 1900 to 1905. Dr. Thomas Tooney claimed to cure all curable diseases using vital magnetism. Dr. Lennox advertised that he cured those suffering with alcoholism and drug addiction. C.H. Bartlett was manager of the institution in 1905.

An associate of Dr. Reed's, Dr. Thomas J. Allen, was formerly physician superintendent of sanitariums at Battle Creek Elmhurst in Chicago. He wrote a column about diet and nutrition called "Daily Health Hints" for a local newspaper. Among his recommendations was a "monodiet," in which one eats only one item during a meal for efficient digestion.

In 1911, Dr. Allen and a group of other interested citizens formed the National Sanitarium Society in order to inform Congress of the fact that the waters of Eureka Springs cured Bright's disease, a kidney ailment. They also wished to "petition the Government in the name of humanity to take charge of the Springs and Reservation to the end that these waters may be preserved in their purity to all mankind." The society also included O.H. Orendorff, Reverend C. N. White, Mrs. Ada C. Kendrick, L.W. McCrory and William Jenkins. Wives of prominent doctors, Mrs. M.R. Regan and Mrs. C.F. Ellis, and newspaper publisher S.A. Diehl were also directors.

Magnetic Spring was deeded to the City of Eureka Springs by Powell Clayton, who was then living in Washington, D.C. As soon as the city acquired the property in 1911, workers set about hand excavating thirty-

Visitors at Magnetic Spring, circa 1915.

eight feet into the side of the mountain to open the main stream of water. A stone and slab-wood structure was built against the cliff face. It covered a pool and gave a cave-like effect.

WATER SHIPPING

When John Tibbs wrote his pamphlet *Joy to the Afflicted Nature's Remedy* in 1882, he claimed that he "Shipped Directly to the Afflicted fresh from the Springs in Barrels, Half Barrels, Kegs, Tin Cans, Cases, Demijohns and Bottles. Boiled, Concentrated and Condensed Water A Specialty."

By 1900, Eureka Water Company was owned by M.F. Gear, who advertised "the Only Carbonating Plant in the City." He claimed that carbonating the water before shipping ensured that it would preserve all of its properties. "I ship water from any of the springs, either carbonated or not, in any quantity that may be desired." F.N. Claflin became partner in the business the following year.[81]

By 1902, William M. Duncan had become owner of many of the Eureka Springs Improvement Company holdings under the name of the Syndicate Company. He initiated modern advertising. For the first time, the brand name Ozarka was associated with Eureka Springs water.

The Ozarka Girl became iconic of the brand, as well as the logo showing the state of Arkansas. As many as twenty-five to thirty rail cars of bottled water and flavored beverages per month were shipped to various towns and cities.

An advertisement in the December 5, 1904 edition of the *Daily Times-Echo* announced that "All Eureka Springs Water is now marketed under the trade name Ozarka."

The Ozarka Girl first appeared in print in 1907.

The Ozarka logo, as shown in the 1907 travelers' edition of the *Times-Echo*.

The same paper included an article that stated, "The great amount of advertising that the Eureka Springs Water Company is sending out daily, is bringing quick returns in almost every case, at the same time it is doing our city a great deal of good." Among the new customers was the British consul in St. Louis.

Another of Duncan's enterprises was the Basin Park Hotel. The property next to Basin Spring stood vacant and in rubble for a period of time after the 1890 fire destroyed the Perry House. Fourteen years later, the building of a new eight-story stone structure began. The hotel opened in 1905 and continues as a hotel today. It was listed in *Ripley's Believe It Or Not!* because all the floors open to ground level on the hillside at the back of the building.

Unfortunately, a terrible national recession claimed much of Duncan's wealth, including his Citizen's Bank, established in 1887 in Eureka Springs. Mr. Duncan cited on July 1, 1907, circumstances beyond his control and "an unprecedented run on the bank" as reason for its closure. Years of receivership followed.

Basin Park Hotel, circa 1905, amidst structures familiar to today's visitors

Over a decade later, shipments of water were twenty-two carloads annually. The head of the Crescent College, Richard R. Thompson, believed the water shipping company could be made into a profitable venture if he focused on marketing to towns where drinking water was "unpalatable or unsatisfactory for other reasons." He set up authorized dealers in cities and towns, especially in the Southwest. Richard Thompson is also known for his renovation of Sanitarium Lake into what became the Lake Lucerne resort.[82]

PALACE BATHHOUSE

Bathhouses have long been a Eureka tradition since the first, started by Thomas Berry Jackson in 1879. The Basin Spring Bathhouse was situated immediately below the Basin Spring and was owned by Eureka Water Company of St. Louis.[83] The building stands today still displaying a sign on the front façade claiming, "Basin Spring has made 90 percent of the cures of Eureka."

Other early bathhouses included the Table Rock Bathhouse on Main Street, which used water from Table Rock Spring (Calef Spring). Gault Bathhouse tapped both Sweet and Harding Springs. These two springs may have also supplied the Nuttall and the American Bathhouses. Named for their sources were Harding, Sweet and Little Eureka Bathhouses.[84]

One of the best known today is the Palace Bathhouse, originally built in 1901 by George T. Williams. Ordinance 300, approved on July 19, 1901, outlined his agreement with the city. Section 1 addressed the laying of pipes under Spring Street to Sweet and Harding Springs, while Section 2 required the payment of three dollars per year per tub in actual use. The city agreed to build reservoirs at each of those springs to hold a "sufficient supply of waste water." The privilege was not exclusive, allowing the city to grant rights to other establishments for bathhouse or bottling purposes. By 1904, in addition to a hotel and baths, the Palace was also home to a laundry, a café and a barbershop.

Nuttall Bathhouse in the foreground and the American Bathhouse in the center, late 1890s.

Mayor Claude A. Fuller and daughters Ruth and Dorothy in front of the Palace Bathhouse, 1911.

A beautification project funded by the Eureka Springs Women's Club in 1916 brought the Waldrup brothers back to Sweet Spring to work more of their stone masonry magic on a design by A.O. Clark, who later designed the auditorium. Improvements included a stone stairway with benches to replace the wooden steps.

RADIOACTIVITY

Lieutenant George N. Chase (retired) of Neosho, Missouri, came to Eureka Springs because he was suffering from Bright's disease, a kidney ailment for which there had been no treatment and of which there were many reported cures due to Eureka Springs water. After he became well, he tested several springs for radioactivity, using a method of exposing photographic plates to radiation. "He placed a number of plates, several of them in air-tight fruit jars, wrapped with several thicknesses of black paper, some under, some above water, in the caves from which the springs flow. In all instances the plates were thoroughly blackened."[85]

After this discovery, radioactivity as a property of the water was reported for several decades. In 1917, one of the world's foremost authorities, Dr. Robert Bell, head of the Battersea London Cancer Hospital and Research

Laboratory, stated, "Brilliant results have been obtained by means of radio-active water, applied internally."[86]

A Commercial Club booklet issued on January 1926 stated:[87]

> *Here the water is radio-active. By drinking it and bathing in it, rheumatic joints, ailing kidneys and other diseased conditions and infections are not only reached and cleansed of poisonous impurities, but a healthy normal activity is reestablished under the influence of that marvelous curative agent known as radium emanations.*

The same booklet went on to say that the tests of Lieutenant Chase were confirmed by Dr. Albert Alleman, United States Army and Navy Museum, and Dr. L.F. Miller, professor of physics, Colorado School of Mines. It further claimed that "the tests demonstrated that the Beta Rays predominate which are considered the most effective in curing diseases of the kidneys."

Chapter 12
GERM THEORY
TAKES HOLD

FROM HORSES TO HORSEPOWER

One guidebook from just after the turn of the century noted that horseback riding was "the conspicuous feature of the pleasure-life of the place." By the 1910s, streetcars, horses and buggies and horseless carriages vied for space on the narrow roads. When a salesman hoping to sell autos to local businessmen drove through town in 1906, he met with a horseback party on Spring Street. "The horses bolted at sight and sound of this very noisy tin carriage and stampeded onto the sidewalks and even through the open doorways of nearby shops." By 1917, twenty-five Eureka residents owned cars. As auto tourism increased, the popularity of railroad passenger service slowed. According to Sam Leath, "By that same year the number of gaited saddle horses for hire had dropped to only about twenty-five."

In 1919, Henry Ford and his family came to Eureka Springs, recognizing the new era for the town and region. Trains still arrived on a fairly regular schedule through 1921 or so, but more and more visitors were depending on the new motor bus service between Eureka Springs and cities in all directions. In 1927, Claude A. Fuller, again elected mayor, succeeded in paving the major streets with concrete at a cost of well over $200,000.

FOR THE PUBLIC GOOD

The United States Public Health Service, which was part of the Department of the Treasury, set the first standards for bacteriological quality in 1914. Regulations began with interstate commerce and quickly generalized to improving the nation's drinking water quality.[88]

Substantial structures
built on the top
four levels of West
Mountain, circa 1915.

Six years after the federal standard was set, an investigation of suspected
cases of typhoid in Eureka Springs was conducted by the Arkansas state health
officer, M.Z. Blair. Between November 1 and December 3, 1920, sixteen
people with typhoid or suspected of having typhoid fever gave histories:

*Most of these cases were visited to determine the possible cause of sickness
and infection the only thing in common which pointed to the probable cause
of illness was spring water. Most of these cases had used either Crescent,
Harding or Sweet Spring water with occasional use of water from Basin
and Magnetic Springs.*

In addition to locals, visitors were said to have suffered from "gastroenteric
disturbances." Bacteriological analysis showed that the water from the
springs was unsafe for drinking, the cause of which was suspected to be
leakage from sewers or septic systems:

Motorized Tally Ho, circa 1910.

All of the watersheds overlying the springs are accessible to persons and animals rendering complete protection of the springs impossible. There can be no doubt that the springs are unsafe sources of drinking water and the city commissioners and acting city health officers were so advised with the advice that the public be warned against using the water.

The city water supply was also checked. The system set up a quarter century earlier was found to be basically good, distributing water to almost all of the population with the exception of part of Main Street. Most residents carried drinking water from the springs for home use.

On December 20, 1920, Dr. C.W. Garrison recommended that a medical health officer be appointed and a competent sanitary engineer employed to prepare a plan for collecting and treating the flow from the larger public springs. The plan would be submitted to the State Board of Health for approval. Among the recommendations was that the public should be warned against the danger of using the spring water by written and oral notice. Additionally, the public water supply should be improved. Apparatus for applying chemical solutions for coagulating bacteria and algae-producing organisms should be placed in service. Chemicals suggested were copper sulfate and aluminum sulfate. Other equipment for filtering the water and disinfecting it with liquid chlorine should be used.

ULTRAVIOLET RAYS

A strange cylindrical structure stands about seven feet tall and five feet in diameter in the park on the north side of the Eureka Springs Historical Museum. This rock hut was used to house equipment for treating the water of Calef Spring and is the only one still existing.

On the recommendation of the state engineer, city commissioners hired the firm of Gannett, Seelye and Flemming to advise them on making the water safe for drinking. The results of the December 1920 water-quality study were confirmed in June 1921. Options proposed were chlorination or electronic sterilization, with the latter being six times more expensive.

Ordinance Number 602 levied a tax for improving and protecting the waters, springs and city reservoirs and for their purification and filtration.[89] The estimated cost was $17,000.[90]

Electronic ultraviolet treatment was chosen over chemical treatment for spring water. By August 15, Dr. Harry M. Hill of the RUV Company of New York City had directed the installation of devices at six springs. Model

Treatment structure at Sweet Spring.

A-1 machines began treating water at Gadd and Calef Springs, and higher-capacity E-1 sterilizers were placed at Basin, Sweet, Harding and Crescent. The machines consisted of a motor generator, which was housed in a structure near the spring, while the RUV machines were housed in "rustic rubble masonry structures" at the spring discharge point.

Flow was measured at 375 gallons per hour under normal conditions and likely increased during wet weather. The E-1 machines were rated at 400 gallons per hour.

In September 1921, a study of the efficiency of the ultraviolet ray treatment was conducted by F.B. Switzer, a bacteriologist with the U.S. Department of Agriculture, and M.Z. Blair, chief sanitary engineer for the Arkansas Board of Health. This showed that the treatment brought about "satisfactory reduction in bacteria and removal of gas producing organisms." The engineers recommended filters to remove the turbidity or muddiness from the water before entering the light treatment area. Treatment at Calef Spring was shown to be ineffective, and it was recommended to abandon it in favor of Magnetic Spring.

In the early to mid-1920s, the Commercial Club promoted tourism, producing booklets such as *Drink from the Fountain of Youth*, *Heart of the Ozarks* and *Drink to Your Health*. These booklets include descriptions of springs and spring water, including its radioactivity and testimonials of people who benefitted from the use of the springs.

The Eureka Springs Chamber of Commerce was established in 1927. Early publications emphasized the beauty of the landscape and the healing springs. That same year, the Mississippi River flooded one-fifth of the state.

In 1928, the auditorium was designed by A.O. Clarke, who had designed Penn Memorial Baptist Church in 1912 and the stonework around Sweet Spring in 1916. The grand opening of the auditorium in 1929 featured John Phillips Sousa and his sixty-seven-piece band. C. Burton Saunders celebrated the occasion by flying over the area in a World War I biplane. Buck had cleared the first trail into the area when his father, Judge Levi Best Saunders, was camped by the Basin Spring. These events corresponded with the fiftieth anniversary of the founding of Eureka Springs and began a tradition of parades and festivals celebrating Eureka's historic heritage.

Chapter 13

WPA AND THE ARTISTS

A s a child, Cora Pinkley-Call lived in the Kings River Valley. In 1904, at age twelve, she was diagnosed with a rare disease, scleroderma. Her arms were becoming hardened, and her doctors feared that the condition would spread over her entire body and eventually kill her. Even at that young age, she knew she wanted to write down the stories that her pioneer grandmothers had told her. When the doctor told her parents that she should be taken out of school and not do anything confining, she was distraught, thinking she would not be able share her stories with other children.

> *A warm spring rain had washed the earth and newly leafed trees gleamed and shone. As I stood looking across the river toward my grandmother's home I saw a double rainbow forming in the sky. They were the brightest rainbows that I have ever seen. I suddenly recalled that the rainbow was the sign of a promise that God had made, never to destroy the earth by water again...Sudden hope sprang into my heart. Nothing was impossible with God...With this hope in my heart I sped toward the little retreat in the pasture where I had buried my little pets and childhood griefs. There in the cedar enclosed little retreat I talked to God. I told Him if He would spare my life, (I didn't ask to be healed) and let me write, that I would give Him the rest of my life; and that I would never forget to give Him the credit for it...I arose from my knees knowing that somehow I was going to reach my goal. I didn't know how a little ignorant hill girl was going to break into print, but I WAS going to do it.*[91]

In *A Stair-Step Town*, published in 1952, she wrote that she had been drinking nothing but Ozarka Water for twelve years and had no trace of the scleroderma. Her hands and arms were supple for the first time in her life.

Descendants of the first settlers. *Left to right, on horseback*: Lewis Harp, Levi Howerton, C. Burton Saunders, L. Jackson and Cora Pinkley-Call (standing).

THE WRITERS' GUILD

During the Great Depression, comedians from the Ozarks made the national scene. The simplicity of the down-home ways of hillbilly characters appealed to radio audiences. Performing over five thousand live radio programs in more than two decades, Chester Lauck and Norris Goff played characters Lum and Abner, as well as many others modeled after people they knew growing up near the town of Waters, Arkansas (renamed Pine Ridge for their show). Another comedian, Bob Burns, who grew up in Van Buren, Arkansas, had his own show in the 1940s featuring the "Arkansas Traveler."

Cora Pinkley-Call started the Ozark Writers' and Artists' Guild to encourage locals to express themselves:

> *Time was when we read about our over exaggerated hill-billy ways and took it lying down, but we don't do that any more for we are creating an art and literature of our own and telling our stories in our own way...tourists following the good highways come here expecting to find the colorful barefoot*

hill-billies, and are disappointed when they find a folk very much like that of any other area.

She wrote *Pioneer Tales of Eureka Springs and Carroll County* (1930), *AR Centennial Historical Pageant* (1936), *Shifting Sands* (1943) and *Dream Garden* (1944). In 1946, she wrote a script for a film about the founding of Eureka Springs. H. William Moore filmed it at Basin Park in October, and descendants of the first families were the actors.

This is my goal when I organized the Ozark Writer-Artist Guild ten years ago and began to advertise the Ozarks, Eureka Springs in particular, as an ideal art and literary center. The Guild was a lusty youngster from the very first, and though it suffered from growing pains, it has strong lungs and is now being heard around the world. Through it many Ozarkans have found a voice, and as we have passed our first decade, I look upon the accomplishments of its members as a proud hen looks upon her brood of chicks.[92]

Among the members of the Writers' Guild were Jesse Russell, May Kennedy McCord, Audra Milum, Bob and Bonnie Lela Crump and Fanny Russ.

Not only did Cora Pinkley-Call help other writers find a voice, but she also gave a voice to many of the area's pioneers. One can just imagine her sitting with her neighbor Mrs. Stites in Mill Hollow and hear the stories flowing. Rebecca Alexander-Stites came to Eureka Springs in 1880. Her father had made his claim the summer the town was founded. She remembered camping on the neighboring 640, the old "Bay's Place." She had set out ivy and calamus roots, and forty some years later they were still coming back each year. Miss Alexander was one of the first students to go to the earliest school at the mouth of Mill Hollow.

Bays Spring was an abundantly flowing spring that was one of the sources of Ozarka Water. During the drought years of the Dust Bowl in Oklahoma, a lot of water was shipped via rail for drinking. Another of the Mill Hollow springs had a fabulous legend of an Indian girl named *Minnehaha*, "Laughing Water," who came to the spring for healing and found both healing and love.

Mill Hollow today is one of those places in town that feels as though you are in the country even though the town has spread to encircle it. Cora Pinkley-Call's log cabin, which was built as her writer's den behind her Mill Hollow home, was moved to Main Street and is now on the grounds of the Eureka Springs Historical Museum.

LAKE LEATHERWOOD

During the Depression, many infrastructure projects were funded to provide jobs. West Leatherwood Creek was the site of one of these that involved the building of a dam and park. The area was not highly populated. Among the landowners were Anthony B. and Andrew S. Fisher, Robert Mullins, Hayes Estate and Florida A. Goddard. A school district for Section 33 was also shown on an engineering map of the project.

In 1938, Lake Leatherwood Dam was built as a Land Utilization Program (LU-AK-21) of the Soil Conservation Service. The dam was 160 feet long, built of concrete covered with hand-cut limestone. A Civilian Conservation Corp (CCC) camp located at the west edge of Berryville was base for the project. In addition to the dam, a bathhouse, swimming and diving area, two arched stone bridges, a caretaker's house and a picnic shelter, built by the CCC, turned the new 100-acre lake into a park for recreation. At 1,600 acres, Leatherwood Park is one of the largest city parks in the United States.

WATER STREET HOLLOW

Another section of town with an abundance of historic springs was Water Street Hollow. No longer actually a road, Water Street is the bottom of a ravine on the east side of Main Street. Douglas and Steele Streets make a loop about midway up the hillside. A variety of styles and periods are reflected in the homes in this area. Corresponding to the elevation of springs in other parts of town, the springs here flow from the level called "the bench" by early settlers and would be later called the upper groundwater system above the Chattanooga shale layer. The historic Water Street area springs include Cave or Maxwell, Little Eureka, Carry A. Nation, East Mountain and Onyx or Laundry Springs.

Little Eureka earned notoriety in 1904 at the St. Louis World's Fair, winning high marks for purity. Carry A. Nation Spring was the nearest spring to the home of the temperance leader who lived across from the spring from 1908 to 1911, when she died. The spring flowed from a cave that was used by residents of East Mountain as a natural icebox. According to Otto Rayburn:

> *This cave has a constant temperature the year 'round and is an ideal natural refrigerator. In the days preceding artificial refrigeration the East Mountain folks made use of Carry's cave for storing milk, butter, and other*

Little Eureka Spring, 1885.

perishables. The water from the cave spring has been piped across the street to Hatchet Hall, which is now a museum and art center, owned by Mr. and Mrs. Louis Freund.

Louis Freund, a Missouri native, studied art in Missouri and Europe and became a professional artist in New York City. When the Depression hit, he was granted commissions by the Works Progress Administration to paint murals on public buildings and scenes of American life in the Arkansas and Missouri Ozarks. Elsie Bates owned a gift shop in Branson, Missouri, and worked as an artist and craftsperson. They met in 1936 and were married three years later in Eureka Springs. In the 1940s, the couple bought Hatchet Hall, Carry Nation's former home on Steele Street. They established the Summer Art School of the Ozarks.

Annual events such as the Ozark Writers' and Artists' Spring Pow-Wow and the Fall Pilgrimage were building Eureka Springs' reputation as a literary and art center. According to Louis Freund, as told to Cora Pinkley-Call:

Mr. Freund has stated that Eureka Springs is not only the most unique town in America, but living costs are quite reasonable here—these qualities

Art School of the Ozarks, annual exhibit in Basin Spring Park, circa 1950s.

Harry Hershey (far right) instructs a painting class visited by Miss Arkansas in 1951. Charlotte Simmen, Elsie Freund (left) and Louis Freund (center) are in attendance.

appeal to most artists, who generally are not equipped with much in the way of worldly goods—particularly art students. Then too, the quiet beauty of the Ozarks is easier to capture on canvass, than the majesty of the Rockies or the varied beauty of the ocean. Pioneer cabins are still to be found in Carroll County and on Saturday afternoons around the court house may still be seen some of the pioneers themselves.[93]

Glenn Ward Dresbach, an internationally known poet, also lived in the hollow. He lived across from Cave Spring from 1941 to 1968.[94]

The following poem was published in *Poetry* in October 1928 and is one of more than forty of Dresbach's works that appeared in this prestigious American journal:[95]

Cave Spring, circa 1880.

THE LITTLE SPRING FLOWS CLEAR AGAIN

The little spring flows clear again
　　While I stand looking close to see
What clouded it. If wings were here
　　To splash the silver merrily
They flew before I came too near.

And if a fawn had rubbed its nose,
　　Thrust deep in silver running cool,
Upon the bottom of the spring
　　It heard me wading in the pool,
Of shadow where the thrushes sing.

The little spring flows clear again,
　　But now is clouded in my mind
The flight of wings that went away—
　　And something that I came to find
Was loveliness afraid to stay.

Where Steele and Flint Streets met, a spring pouring from a small cave became known as Onyx Spring. Jewelry makers such as Charles

Onyx Spring, circa 1925.

Stehm made souvenirs from the stone. This spring was also known as Laundry Spring.

One of the earliest ordinances, about 1880, specified that "all persons washing their persons or clothes in or above the basins of all public springs shall be guilty of a misdemeanor." After the spring water flowed beyond the immediate discharge point, it was often collected for the purpose of bathing or washing clothes. In Kalklosch's 1881 guidebook, there was a "Laundry Spring" in the area that is now Black Bass Lake.

In the Water Street area, runoff from several springs flowed down over the rock ledges to the creek. Accessible for household use, this wastewater was collected, and a washhouse or laundry was established. Many women listed their occupations as laundress.

In 1922, residents of East Mountain raised all the funds needed to employ carpenters, Dillow and Bingham, to build a wood shelter over the cave opening. It was proudly boasted, "Not a penny came from the city for these improvements."

Laundry Spring Reservation was established early and appears on the 1893 Riley plat map. A detailed definition of the boundaries was written into law in 1903. The reservation was included as part of the contiguous lands that formed Water Street Park when it was established by Mayor Marcile Davis in 1980.

Old Soldier Spring flowed from a small cave near Copper Street on East Mountain, not far from the Water Street area:

> *According to legend, two bushwackers were killed at the entrance of this cave by federal soldiers during the Civil War. A bushwacker is an outlawish fellow who hides under a bush and takes a "whack" at you with his rifle gun. In this instance the soldiers got the first whack and the stream from the cave was named Soldier Spring. For several years the large oak tree across the road from the spring was a natural bee tree and a swarm of honey-makers occupied it each season. Not many modern towns can boast of a bee tree within the city limits.* [96]

Cold Spring, also known as Cold Water Spring and Stites Spring, was located at Breeding and Alexander Streets not far from Old Soldier Spring. It was surveyed as early as 1881 in North Eureka, its reservation established by ordinance in 1882. Mr. Breeding was an alderman at the time. According to Kalklosch, "The Cold Water Spring, near the Iron and Sulphur, is supposed to be free from any unusual characteristic, and is used to counteract the

Old Soldier Spring, 1976.

too rigid action of the others in some cases of prostration." It was among the primary spring reservations made official in 1886 after the town site ownership was legally recognized.

In the late 1940s, property owners in the Breeding Block were given an easement to supply water from Cold Spring until city water mains were brought into that section of town.[97] In the 1980s, the spring discharged through a pipe into a rock-filled barrel, where it disappeared into the ground again. Hydrologists were told that the spring originally flowed from the hill thirty feet above the site, but blasting had caused a change in its channels. At that time, it was providing domestic water to the Duffy household.[98]

Chapter 14
STAIR STEPS AND PICKET FENCES

A fter World War II, people craved an affirmation of life. Scientists searched for its building blocks, confirming that DNA held the genetic code and discovering its double-helix shape. A baby boom combined with improved medical care, medicines and sanitation led to an increase in human population. The white picket fence was truly a symbol of family and aspirations of people to settle into a good life. In 1952, Cora Pinkley-Call published *A Stair-Step Town*, which appealed to those looking back to the town's origin, as well as those looking forward to the future.

Eureka Springs' youths played baseball in the middle of Spring Street. "I remember as a kid we used to play around Grotto Spring or Crescent Spring…That was our territory, Library to Grotto," recalled Eureka native Nancy Clark.[99]

People continued to drink from the springs according to Pat Rhiel Jones and her sister-in-law, Sue Cole Jones:

> *Grotto Spring was our closest spring, and we carried water from there, my grandmother drank water from one of the springs on East Mountain, and I think it was known as Soldier Spring, and we would stop and get her drinking water for her as most people did back then was carry water from a spring.*

According to Sue:

> *We had a spring on our place called Bell Spring and it was called Bell Spring because you could hear a little bell back in the cave where the spring came out of. And one time a gentleman went up and disturbed whatever it was that was causing the bell to ring and there was no longer a bell sound*

out of the spring. That's where we got our drinking water for the house. And it came down to the house by gravity. Daddy had built a five hundred gallon tank and it would flow from the spring to the tank and from the tank down to the house, and that's how got our water.[100]

People traveled to places where they could enjoy the natural environment. Mrs. Evan Booth, who owned Blue Spring a few miles outside town, opened it to the public. Mount Aire, established as Camp Leath in the 1920s, was popular with tourists who wanted to stay in a rustic cabin, tent or recreational vehicle. Harpers and Eureka Courts provided individual lodging in small modern cottages complete with the white picket fence.

OZARKA

Richard Thompson was invited to speak at a conference of the Texas Bottled Water Dealers Convention in March 1956. As president of Eureka Springs Water Company, he had a lot of firsthand information about the water shipping business:

Today we ship over three hundred cars per annum or a total of above three million gallons approximately 1/3 of which is shipped from Hot Springs similar in mineral analysis; but as intimated elsewhere in my talk, the surface hardly has been scratched because there are so many towns and cities where the people need and want a quality drinking water instead of being compelled to drink the water from the tap, which in most instances is treated so heavily that the taste is unpalatable; and as more intelligent people recognize, the chemicals are harmful.

I shall be glad to give you a picture of my operations. The spring is situated up the mountains about two miles distant from the railroad tracks, and the water flows through a two-inch galvanized pipe line leading from the springs to the track. Formerly we used our own glass-lined tank cars, but as these wore out we began to lease tank cars. These are lined with a little-known product made in England called Tetley's Enamel, which hardens like glass. The cost of lining each of these cars varies from five hundred to one thousand dollars each. The water comes down to the loading point with a gravity pressure of about 50 pounds; and with that pressure it is filtered first through sand, then through composition stone, and then a polishing filter paper. It is not otherwise treated.

Ozarka Water railroad boxcars and tank car on the tracks by the railway depot, 1961.

Thompson marketed the water for its pleasant taste, and he knew that many people drank it for its health benefits. He believed in its value, especially in the case of kidney and bladder stones.

> *I have argued with the leaders of the town that the Town of Eureka Springs possessed many features which other Ozark resorts cannot claim and that we should reestablish Eureka Spring as a health resort rather than a vacation spot. There are a limited number of citizens in Eureka Springs who agree with me but the younger generation and the horde of outsiders who have come to the town do not seem to agree with me. I have known literally hundreds, perhaps thousands, who have come to Eureka Springs and who have been restored to health after suffering for many years from disorders of the kidney, bladder and stomach and many of them came in on stretchers.*

OZARK FOLKLORE

The first folklore conference in Arkansas was held in Eureka Springs in 1928. The event was organized by Sam Leath, Vance Randolph and Samuel Dellinger, "grandfather of Arkansas archeology." Dellinger had been inspired by M.R. Harrington's finds in rock shelters around the Ozarks in the early

1920s and wanted to ensure that native artifacts were properly collected so that prehistoric peoples could be understood. He worked tirelessly excavating shelters in the White River region that are now under Beaver Lake.

Dellinger returned to Eureka Springs to participate in a Folklore Festival in March 1934. The event featured a musical "round table" by twenty musicians seated in a circle, each playing a different tune at the same time. A husband-calling contest and demonstrations of weaving and knitting by local artists, as well as cotton ginning, carding and spinning by Mrs. Darrow, were topped off by dinner and an evening of entertainment.

Otto Ernest Rayburn fell in love with the Ozarks as a young man. "A lubber from the level lands" of Iowa and Kansas, he moved to Reed Spring, Missouri, in 1917, about which he wrote:

> *That big spring tumbling from the bowels of the earth in the center of the crazy-quilt town! A million gallons or more of crystal clear water each twenty-four hours! It was one of the first large springs I had seen and my eyes were as big as a giant's pocket watch. I picked up a tin cup and drank to my fill. It is an old tradition that if you take three drinks from an Ozark spring you will always return for more. I drank and became an adopted Ozarker.*

Twenty-nine years later, after he retired from teaching, he moved to Eureka Springs, where he opened a bookstore specializing in Ozark folklore. Soon after arriving, Rayburn pitched his idea for promoting Eureka Springs as a pioneer village complete with log buildings, crafts and live demonstrations. The civic clubs and the chamber of commerce were not responsive to the idea, the population thinking of themselves in a much different light. In time, Silver Dollar City in southern Missouri combined preservation with a commercial theme park, and later Mountain View picked up the idea and developed its Ozark Folk Center with public funding.

In 1952, Rayburn took over management of the Ozark Folk Festival. The program included traditional songs by the Ozark Choral Club; a square dance exhibition; a fiddling contest with prizes of fifteen, ten and five dollars; a zither solo; and performances by some of the big names of Ozark regional folk singing: Booth Campbell, Doney Hammontree and Fred High and his sister, Mary Brisco.

The *Eureka Springs Story* was published in 1954, and Rayburn's autobiography, *Forty Years in the Ozarks*, came out three years later. The *Ozark Folk Encyclopedia* was Rayburn's retirement project, consisting of 229 "volumes" of loose-leaf binders—his collection of pamphlets, clippings, photos, maps and other materials that he used as source material.[101] These are preserved in the Special Collections at the University of Arkansas. One such article showed the Ozark Hillfolks Club cleaning up Soldier Spring in December 1959 as a community service project.

ALPINE HIKING CLUB

Walking the hills had long been a popular activity. In the late 1960s, Eurekans formed the Alpine Hiking Club, which was documented in the newspaper by Virginia Tyler in a column called "Hiking Club Highlights." Tyler's descriptions of their adventures give wonderful details about some of the beautiful sites they visited over a twenty-year period. The following are a few excerpts from her early columns:

What a wonderful rainy day was last Sunday, and although the clouds were heavy, the hikers were light-hearted and had a grand time on their return trip to Hyde Hollow and Moss Spring. This is a magnificent hike in any kind of weather; its especially nice when the sun is shining—but even when you can hear the pitter-patter of the warm summer rain on the leaves of the tall oak trees going down into the valley—it's still delightful (June 25, 1967).

Moss Spring is just fantastic. The water comes down over two moss-covered bluffs—and when the sun shines through the water and the moss—it looks like sparkling diamonds on a setting of green velvet. It's a fairyland, I tell you (November 24, 1968).

Although the April skies were rather drippy, last Sunday, fifteen enthusiastic members of the Alpine Hiking Club, hiked down the woodsy lane that leads to Thompson's Spring from the Statue road. There's a mystic fascination about the new-leafed forest on a rainy day, like this was, and we were a chipper group as we jauntily walked along, dressed appropriately for any kind of weather.

It's a delightful hike down this rustic road. We came to an old dilapidated house, built between two craggy bluffs, that we had much fun exploring. We wondered who lived here long ago. Around this house was an old weatherworn fence and Alys Reeder informed us it was called a "paling" fence. You learn things on these hikes!

Moss Spring, 1880.

On down the hill we hiked until we came to a rocky stream bed, with the clear, fresh water rushing along. Crossing this on stepping stones, and around the bend we came to Thompson Spring—a beautiful place with wild ferns growing in profusion around the gushing water. Did you know that this water is shipped all over the country?

We had two Elmers on this jaunt—Elmer Sleade, who is a vigorous member of the Club, and Elmer Roberts, our four-legged mascot! Elmer Roberts hasn't hiked with us for several Sundays—he's has been courting a little Beagle, who lives up on Prospect Avenue (April 21, 1968).

We hiked for about an hour up this rugged valley; crossing the creekbed many times until we came to Thompson Spring. The foliage was so dense around the spring, we could hardly see it, but Doug Sleade crossed the creek and in the fresh-flowing water of the spring, found the nicest growth of water cress which we had fun picking (August 11, 1968).

It was a clear, cold December night last Sunday, as the Alpine Hiking Club hiked around town, lustily singing the traditional Christmas Carols for our own enjoyment, as well as for the nice folks along the way!

We left the New Orleans at five p.m.—there were eleven of us, including Dwayne and Darwin Jones, two of the youngest members of the Hiking Club. We hiked for about an hour around Spring Street, up Ellis Grade, around Prospect and down Pine Street to town again.

Passing Grotto Spring, we descended down into this cave for a few minutes to get warm—and it so resembled the Creche where Christ was born, that we very reverently sang, "Away In a Manger" with no one to hear it, but just us! It was truly inspirational!

Looking up at the clear night sky, there was a brand new moon and a big sparkling star close to it. We all imagined it was Apollo 8 on its way to the moon—and it might well have been (December 22, 1968)!

The photo of the earth from space taken on that mission became a rallying symbol for the first Earth Day in 1970. The hikers often shared current events, as well as historic facts and legends, along the trail:

Mose and Erin Hyde were brothers and itinerate preachers and their homes were down in this valley [Hyde Hollow]. *They both raised large families and, many years ago, everybody in the countryside knew the attractive Hyde girls! All that is left now of the old homestead is the small cave where they kept their milk, butter and vegetables (November 24, 1968).*

Years ago; when Dr. Pearl Tatman was a prominent lady physician in Eureka Springs, she used to ride horseback from her country home in a valley near Onyx Cave Road, over this rustic route, through Stock Pen Hollow, to the Old Magnetic Hollow road and then into town to visit her many patients. Everybody loved Dr. Pearl—there was never a night too cold or dark or rainy that she wouldn't come when called; and this valley was a shortcut to town that she always took—riding her faithful horse—her medicine in her saddle bags (June 1, 1969).

Chapter 15

THE CENTENNIAL

A fire in 1958 gutted the stone structure on Spring Street known as the Sanford Building. For twenty years, the scorched, rotted timbers stood as testimony of decline. The town had survived low ebbs four times in its history, first when the railroad moved its operation to Harrison in 1913. The other three were worldwide events: the two world wars and the Great Depression.

In the 1960s, Gerald and Elna Smith were seeking to settle somewhere. They bought Penn Castle and began to restore it. Mr. Smith had a vision to build a monument to the Lord. He wanted a hilltop property with a spring on it. When the mountain across the valley became available, he made an "X" on the ground and said, "Charles, this is where we are going to erect a seven-story statue of Jesus Christ, the monument to my Savior that I've always wanted to build." Sculptor Emmet Sullivan was hired to design and build the statue that was called *Christ of the Ozarks* in 1966. Two years later, the *Great Passion Play* began on top of Magnetic Mountain, named for the spring in the valley below.[102]

Another boost to the economy was Beaver Lake. The dam was completed in 1966, and the reservoir was filled to normal operational level over the next two years. Named for Wilson Ashbury Beaver, a contemporary of Alvah Jackson and Levi Best Saunders, the lake was a U.S. Army Corps of Engineers Project. It was the fourth dam built in the White River Basin since the Flood Control Act of 1938. It was also one of the first Army Corps reservoirs to be authorized for municipal and industrial water supply. When the Beaver Land Office opened in 1959 to acquire land, investors and developers began to purchase large tracts that could later be subdivided.

The project was not without challenges. Congress passed the appropriation of funds over President Eisenhower's veto in 1960. Shortly after the building began, a large cavern was discovered upstream that had to be filled with two hundred cubic yards of grout material. In addition to flood control and recreation, the reservoir would also provide a source of drinking water to surrounding communities, some of the fastest growing to the west in the Northwest Arkansas Corridor. Electric power generation began in 1965.

Ozarka Water shipped its last spring water from Eureka Springs shortly after the death of Richard Thompson. After the railroad had ended service to town, Thompson continued to ship by tanker truck to distributors in the Southwest. Eventually, he sold the company to Arrowhead, which moved operations to California in 1967. The end of one era was the beginning of another.

PLANNING AND PRESERVATION

On March 17, 1966, the people of Eureka Springs voted on and passed Ordinance 871, which created a planning commission. After a planning process, with assistance from consultants from the University of Arkansas, the planning commission voted to create a historic district. On December 18, 1970, the Eureka Springs Historic District was placed on the National Historic Register. The Historic District boundaries were the same as the city's boundaries at that time.

The 1970s was a decade of change not only for Eureka Springs and northwest Arkansas but also for the country. In national affairs, the Environmental Protection Agency began operation. By 1972, the Clean Water Act forbidding discharges of pollutants into navigable waters had been passed. Nixon stumbled and fell through the Watergate scandal. The middle of the decade brought the United States bicentennial and a renewed interest in nostalgia and history.

On the local front, the Carroll County Water District was set up, with Charles Burton Freeman as director. After the Clean Water Act was passed, the city began its 201 planning process for wastewater management. June Westphal and Catherine Osterhage published *A Fame Not Easily Forgotten: An Autobiography of Eureka Springs*, and in 1971, the Eureka Springs Historical Museum was founded.

In January 1972, a nineteen-year-old "washed up onto the shores of Eureka Springs." Crescent Dragonwagon described her first impressions:

> *From my first walk in the town that would become my home, how moving and timeless the narrow street seemed, curving uphill, with its Victorian*

stone buildings. The old city was deserted, its out-of-time, peculiar atmosphere as palpable as the needle-fine rain misting my face that day under a gray sky.

Remember, it was January 1972. Deep off-season. What few shops existed, in that preboom, prerenovation-conscious Eureka, were closed. There were almost no people on the street, which was why I was puzzled by some faint, convivial sounds coming from somewhere unseen. Just as I reached the bend that curves Spring Street into a sinuous traffic-slowing angle, I saw a single illuminated shop, from which the sounds were issuing. Butter-yellow light poured from the plate-glass window, the sole luminescence that gray afternoon on the empty archaic street. That, and the sounds, drew me into the tiny coffee shop, long, narrow, filled with conversation, laughter, someone playing the guitar. It was aromatic, steamy from an enormous brass-and-copper espresso machine, and filled with eight or ten people, mostly young, long-haired, in denim.

The same year, Robert "Butch" Berry returned to Eureka Springs after having grown up playing among the springs, woods, unique structures and underground tunnels. His grandmother, who had raised him after his parents died in a tragic accident, needed assistance. Mayor Fred Naff immediately invited him to be on the planning commission. His mentor in college had

The Rosalie after restoration. Postcard invitation to the Open House, 1975.

been Dr. Cyrus Sutherland, professor of architecture and a leader in historic preservation in Arkansas. Berry would provide valuable information to residents and business owners as they became enthusiastic about restoration of the town as its 100th anniversary approached.[103]

CENTENNIAL COMMISSION

At the end of 1977, the city council set up a special commission to organize events celebrating the city's centennial year of 1979. According to John Cross, while he was away hunting, he was appointed co-chair of the commission along with Steve Chyrchel: "The whole centennial to me was taking care of what we've got and bringing back what we've lost. That was the whole theme of it. The 'dance with what brung ya'…with the springs, but that was the whole theme, taking care of what we've got, taking care of the springs."[104]

A Springs Committee of the Centennial Commission was chaired by Phillip Bullock. Civic organizations were organized to adopt and develop restoration projects for the grounds around the principal springs.

Both my grandparents on both sides moved here because of the healing waters, so it doesn't speak too well for my genetics if they both felt like they were ill when they moved here and had to bathe in the water, so anyway my father lived to be 91 years old…and my mom…88, so apparently whatever worked in the water worked pretty well.[105]

Bullock proposed the idea for a City Parks Commission that would be responsible for the upkeep of the springs. In 1981, the Eureka Springs Parks and Recreation Commission was established to maintain the city-owned spring reservations and parks.

Restoration efforts were community wide. Representatives of the Centennial Commission approached county judge Wayne Farwell, asking him to restore the Carroll County Western District Courthouse, built in 1907 in downtown Eureka Springs. The Historic District Commission was established in 1978. Original members were Jeannette Rosewater Bullock, Ruth Perry Eichor, June Johnson Westphal, Cecil Walker, Cleo Miller and Charles Burton Freeman. The Eureka Springs Preservation Society, an association of private owners of historic properties, was organized the same year.

In February 1979, the Preservation Society was awarded a grant to conduct a survey of all structures within the Historic District. It found over one thousand buildings and only 1,700 permanent residents. Butch Berry offered workshops designed to give homeowners the basic tools and background to help them make the best choices to restore and preserve their historic homes.

According to John Cross, he and the Bank of Eureka Springs were leading by example, by restoring many buildings that they owned and by constructing their new bank in a style and with materials reflecting the Victorian traditions of the Historic District. "No carnivalizing," he said. The people wanted to bring back what had once been, such as the trolleys, train and streetlights resembling earlier times.

A huge ice storm froze out the opening ceremony, which was to be held on New Year's Day. Two months later, the proclamation was officially read, and a flag was raised to open the festivities.

Several events started during the centennial year have continued, such as the Victorian Classic Run and the Tour of Homes. A large outdoor mural was designed by Louis Freund and painted by local artists under his direction. Native Eurekans were celebrated with a special event and a huge old-fashioned Fourth of July parade that was led by Centennial Commission co-chairmen John Cross and Steve Chyrchel. A costumed Victorian Ball at the Crescent Hotel brought the year's events to a close. The Centennial Commission sponsored the publication of *A Postcard History of Eureka Springs* and issued souvenir collectors' plates featuring an artist drawing of Crescent Spring.

Something Stirring Downstream

In the midst of the celebration of the one-hundred-year-old health resort that was founded on the springs, many citizens expressed their strong concerns about the realistic, everyday problems of living in this unique landscape. A headline in the March 1, 1979 *Daily Times-Echo* read, "Sewer plant location tops council agenda." An engineering study had estimated that out of every 100,000 gallons of sewage produced at the treatment facility on Leatherwood Creek, more than 50,000 gallons escape before reaching the facility. A detailed system evaluation had been completed. The city was finally within reach of acquiring federal funds for a new wastewater treatment system when the city's downstream neighbors organized a movement to oppose the plan. According to Pat Costner in *We All Live Downstream*:

The city's rural neighbors and their urban sympathizers organized the community's first public eco-political group, "Concerned Citizens." They carried their cause to the media, state agencies, and then to the Environmental Protection Agency (EPA). After months of relentless effort, the suggestion percolated down to city officials to pick another spot for the their new treatment facility.

The area's first grass-roots environmental group renamed itself Concerned Citizens' National Water Center. It questioned the city and its engineers about why they were using a treatment process that had failed many times in other areas of the limestone plateaus of which Eureka Springs was a part. They educated themselves about the geologic and hydrologic characteristics that included the abundance of springs and began to seek alternatives that could lead to the end of their contamination.

Chapter 16

HEAL THE WATERS

Heal the water as she has healed you
Heal the water it's the least you can do
For all the life she's given you
Imagine her beautiful and make it come true.

There is a reason for coming together
Like a cloud in a summer rain
There is a reason for coming together
To shower our love and make her clean again.[106]
—Don Matt

LEAKY PIPES

In the early 1980s, water issues were constantly in the news, emotions ran high
and much was learned about the springs. Doug Stowe expressed it this way:

> *Springs are a connection between us, because you have someone polluting*
> *the springs at one end, and you have someone attempting to drink from the*
> *springs at the other, and so I realized, that the springs were a failing in our*
> *efforts to take care of each other.*[107]

In April 1980, the city completed a facility plan for wastewater treatment
in compliance with Section 201 of the Clean Water Act. Uproar over the
plan resulted in a community-wide effort to revise it and to seek alternatives.
Federal funds for a major coordinated effort to complete the design phase

were secured from the Environmental Protection Agency. Five main tasks would be carried out: 1) location of sampling sites; 2) establishment of baseline conditions for water quality, geologic, hydrologic and biological setting; 3) analysis and evaluation of the water quality and biological impacts of exfiltrated sewage; 4) preparation of draft and final reports; and 5) public participation.

The city's conventional gravity sewage collection system and trickling filter treatment plant were in need of updating. Broken lines allowed sewage to seep out and contaminate the springs. The twenty-six-year-old plant overflowed during some storms when rainwater and groundwater entered the system. While most of the pipes were installed in 1956, many were holdovers from 1894.

A festival provided a way for citizens to celebrate, as well as to network and share information. Governor Bill Clinton signed a proclamation declaring that September 22–29 was "Heal the Waters Week":

WHEREAS, *The Earth's waters are a vital part of man's existence; and*
WHEREAS, *Through all our lives the waters have sustained, nurtured and even healed our bodies and spirits; and*
WHEREAS, *We realize that while we continually strive to develop new technologies to deal with our problems, the greatest innovation is conservation; as we conserve precious water, we can also conserve and enrich our soil through recovery of some waste; and*
WHEREAS, *All over the Earth the rivers, lakes and oceans have struggled to cleanse themselves of waste, but can do so no longer by themselves; we must join with them to conserve, protect, and Heal the Waters;*
NOW, THEREFORE, *I, Bill Clinton, Governor of the State of Arkansas do hereby proclaim September 22 through 29, 1980, as*
HEAL THE WATERS WEEK
in Arkansas to celebrate and cherish the waters of our Earth, and to rededicate ourselves to the protection of those waters.
IN WITNESS WHEREOF, *I have hereunto set my hand and caused the Great Seal of the State of Arkansas to be affixed at the Capitol in Little Rock on this 25ᵗʰ day of August in the year of our Lord nineteen hundred eighty.*
Bill Clinton
GOVERNOR

Not unlike one hundred years earlier, water was the major topic in town. The heritage of miraculous cures remained close to the hearts of Eureka's people. A slate of candidates for the city council campaigned with promises to repair all the leaking pipes and to renovate the wastewater plant.

Frankie Stephens was a graduate student working on his masters in civil engineering at the University of Arkansas under Dr. Dee. T. Mitchell. He conducted preliminary water-quality testing in December 1980. He located ninety sources, including eighty-two springs, six seeps and two wells. On-site tests measured flow rate, water temperature, dissolved oxygen, pH and specific conductance at more than half of the springs that were identified. Others were dry or had too little flow. An additional seventeen springs were either inaccessible to direct flow or excluded because testing might have an impact on the site. Two of the springs were at the bottom of a lake, and two were not tested because permission was denied.

As a requirement of the EPA grant, an initial public meeting was held on January 15, 1981.[108] June Westphal, member of city council, opened with a brief welcoming statement and introduced Vernon Rowe of McClelland Engineering. He introduced other members of the team. They were Frankie Stephens; Khan Hussain from Comprehensive Planning Institute; Dr. Tom Aley, president of Ozark Underground Laboratory; Dan Hoffman, another hydrologist; and Dr. Hugh Jeffus and Dr. Dee Mitchell from Environmental Engineers, Inc., a Springdale company specializing in wastewater.

"My hope is that what you'll have is a document that will be of value not only to this project but to other things in the future," said Tom Aley, who would be the chief hydrologist for the exfiltration study.[109]

Vernon Rowe announced that the city should form a Citizens Advisory Committee (CAC) and stated that there was money for a public participation coordinator who would be a liaison between the CAC and the engineers. In order to be ready for the rainy season, the committee should be chosen right away.

After the initial meeting, the city council selected individuals to lead the Citizen's Advisory Committee as public participation coordinators: Pat Pinkley (now Costner), Barbara Hovland (now Harmony) and Jacqualine Froelich. The committee met every two weeks from March 1981 to February 1982. Members conducted a tourist survey and a door-to-door canvass. They kept on top of the data being collected and explored options, including fixing pipes, user fees and composting toilets. According to Pat Costner, there was

so much public involvement, everybody in the community, no matter what their political, economic, class, whatever it was, knew about the whole issue had opinions about it, was involved, most likely directly one way or another, so that it just unified the community in, I think, a totally unprecedented way.[110]

SAMPLING AND TESTING

The springs were classified by use. Thirty-six springs were undeveloped or in a natural state, while nineteen had once been developed but were now abandoned. Others were listed as public or private. Nine public springs with tourist attraction but unavailable for drinking were: Basin, Ice Cream Seep, Sweet, Harding, Crescent, Grotto, Clear, Mystic and Carrie Nation. Seven public springs with tourist attraction that were available for drinking purposes were Calef, Magnetic, Cave, Little Eureka, Onyx-Laundry, Cold-Stites and Fish Pond. Private springs serving as drinking water sources in homes or businesses included Living Water, Bay, Ethridge, Bancroft Lodge, Robertson and Taff. Thirteen private springs were used to water stock and as ponds or fountains.

Conventional water-quality samples were collected periodically from March through May and analyzed in the laboratory. Tests were done for ammonia nitrate-nitrogen, chloride, total phosphorus, surfactants, total organic carbon, total and fecal coliform and fecal streptococcus.

In April, Ozark Underground Laboratory began groundwater hydrology work. While the Chattanooga shale and Boone limestone layers were mentioned in the 1921 Health Department report, these layers and others were explained in more detail in the 1981 study.

DYE TRACING

Dye tests were conducted for groundwater tracing and to detect the presence of contamination. Tracer dyes were injected at seven manholes in various parts of the system. An estimated 40 percent of the wastewater was leaking into the groundwater. An eighth test dye was placed in a losing stream, a stream that flows on the surface and then disappears into the subsurface. This was to test an area where there were no sewer lines. Approximately 130 to 140 residences and businesses within the city limits used individual soil absorption systems, septic tanks and leach fields. Septic fields that require sufficient soil for filtration were found to be even worse than broken pipes.

A second type of dye test measured optical brightener levels in spring water. Found in many laundry detergents, optical brighteners were fluorescent white dyes used to intensify the whiteness of clothes. Their presence or absence indicated water contamination from sewage. On April 10, specially prepared un-whitened cotton samplers were placed in the flow of fourteen sites. Near Cardinal Spring, the results were strongly positive within fifteen minutes. At the sewer plant, the test was strongly positive in five hours, while farther upstream on Leatherwood Creek, immediately above the sewer plant, a weakly positive result occurred at five hours. The rest of the samplers remained in the springs for about a week. Two were not detectable: Johnson and Ozarka Springs. All the other sites were positive. Several springs were found to be the home of Ozark blind salamanders; however, springs that ranked highest for optical brighteners did not appear to provide good habitat for this species.

RECHARGE ZONES

In the exfiltration study, hydrologists clarified the underground workings of the springs by describing the groundwater systems, tracing their flow and delineating and mapping the recharge areas of seventy-six springs. The myth that the spring water came from great distances, such as hundreds of miles, was dispelled. It became clear that water passing into the ground in the area where most townspeople lived eventually arrived at one or more of the springs. In the final report for the study, chief hydrologist Tom Aley stated, "The various sources of unchecked pollution within the City of Eureka Springs ultimately find their way to the City's spring systems." The bright side of this, according to Aley, was that "in this setting, periodic sampling of the springs under a continuing monitoring program to detect the presence of sewage contamination is a reasonable and cost-effective approach for identifying leakage problems." Thus, it was important to locate the recharge areas for each spring. "The recharge area of a spring is that region where waters sinking into the ground will ultimately be discharged from the spring in question."

Groundwater traces, relative flow rates and water-quality information were used to delineate individual recharge areas. The location and structure of the Chattanooga shale was a major geologic factor because this layer separated groundwater into an upper and lower system. This was also given as a reason for the large number of small springs in the study area. Due to its lack of permeability, the contours on the top of the Chattanooga shale, which may be different from the surface topography, direct the flow of water across it in the upper groundwater system.

Sweet Spring's recharge area was based on the results of four of the eight dye traces that were done. Several storm events occurred during the sampling

PLATE 5.2
COMPOSITE RECHARGE AREAS FOR ALL MAJOR SPRINGS

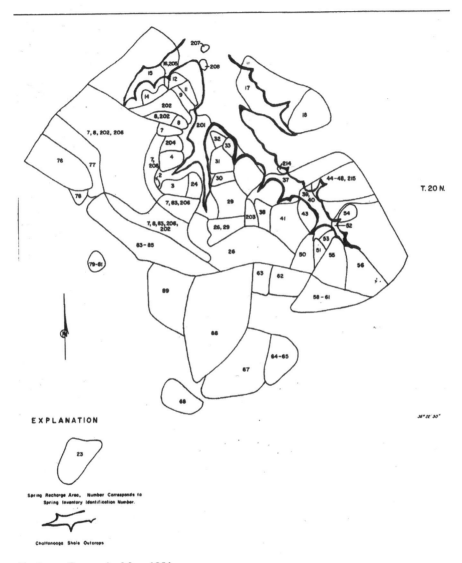

Recharge Composite Map, 1981.

so that the flow was good, usually peaking the same day. One might expect the area directly above the spring to recharge it. This area was protected as a spring reservation in the 1880s. The actual recharge area is much larger. The recharge zone mapped in the study included much of Singleton Street, the upper historic loop, Eureka Springs Hospital and sections of Highway 62 near Planer Hill and Dairy Hollow to Pivot Rock Road. Leaky pipes in the gully behind the homes on Wall Street or the shops in the Quarter could contribute to Sweet Spring, as well as Harding, Arsenic or Cave Springs.

The study clearly indicated that the land on which the entire city is built, except the deepest valleys below the level of the springs, contributes water to their flow. A composite map showed the recharge zones of seventy-six springs in the study area.

New terms were introduced and became part of the local vocabulary as people struggled, studied and debated trying to understand the unique challenges of limestone geology. Areas where water moved quickly into the subsurface through openings such as sink holes or losing streams were known as discrete recharge zones. Areas with enough overlying soils to permit slow percolation of water into the subsurface, diffuse recharge zones, are rare in these hills. Most of the groundwater recharge in the Eureka Springs area was through discrete recharge zones.

"TRICKLE-DOWN ECONOMICS"

The Citizen Advisory Committee conducted a door-to-door survey in order to map the wastewater collection system and identify sources of pollution. Teams of one adult and one high school student knocked on doors asking about water usage, conservation and waste disposal. A survey of tourists was also conducted. Citizens were asked to pass on their concerns and advice to the city officials. On the top of the list were speedy resolution to the wastewater collection and treatment problem and an equitable user charge system. Consultants agreed, stating in their report:

> On the social scene, the concern about an equitable user-charge system strikes at the heart of all major issues surrounding the 201 project. There is no doubt that to solve all the water quality problems would cost money. While the EPA is expected to provide 75% of the funds for eligible items, to generate the local share of 25% from conventional sources would not be an easy task. In a town where the people's income on a per capita basis is only two-thirds the national average and in a town where the tourists outnumber the local population by a margin of almost 2 to 1 during peak months, a user-charge system has the seeds of becoming grossly unfair to the average people.[111]

The report concluded:

Because the wastewater project has to be designed to handle the waste from tourists and local people alike, it is only fair to say that the tourists must bear their prorated share of the cost…if this concept of cost burden is introduced in the design of a user-charge system then that would be a socially equitable system.

By the late summer of 1981, the water center staff were evicted from their city hall office, their files impounded and salaries withheld. The Citizen Advisory Committee concluded that appropriate on-site systems were the most economical solution. A decentralized approach was favored.

The final report of the exfiltration study outlined a short-term and long-term program to restore the springs, concluding with the following:

The 201 program for Eureka Springs began about 8 years ago. It has had its ups and downs. Concerns and disagreements on various issues have had their peaks and valleys. But never in the history of this community a more momentous time has come than now to work cooperatively to promote common goals for the water quality in general, and the spring systems restoration in particular. If such a cooperative spirit can be developed to foster community goodwill, then the days of "healing waters" will be here again.[112]

When Vernon Rowe announced the city's new plan at a public hearing in April 1982, no one was satisfied. Many citizens who had been very involved were shut out as the city ended the planning stage.

By 1983, the Arkansas Health Department responded to a boom in construction of new motels by ordering Building Inspector Charles Fargo to stop issuing building permits for projects that would need to connect to the sewer system.

The Reagan administration attempted to roll back the Clean Air and Clean Water Acts of the previous two decades, while the city had difficulty getting EPA reimbursements for the planning stage and federal funding for the new plant.

Tensions increased, and activists spoke out. "But now there's a sign saying the water is bad and I won't be blind anymore because now I'm just mad," was a line from a song by local musician Terry Bradt. Today, environmental issues have become mainstream, and environmental science is taught in school, but it was not always that way.

The National Water Center's *We All Live Downstream: A Guide to Waste Treatment that Stops Water Pollution* was published in 1986. It summarized the water crisis and featured information about composting toilets, arguing that the crisis is not a lack of water but a lack of clean water and that "water toilets foster the illusion that these and any other products can be flushed away without consequences." Chapter eight, "Water Lessons that Travel," summarized the Public Participation Program and other campaigns that followed, including an effort by citizens to block the reclassification of Leatherwood Creek as "effluent- dominated." Leatherwood Creek Watershed is now recognized as having one of the first watershed groups in Arkansas.

Pat Costner, after a long career as an authority on environmental and water-quality issues, reflected on this period thirty years later:

> *One third of them* [residents] *agreed that they were willing to go to appropriate onsite treatment systems…in an effort to clean up the springs and keep them clean…I get chill bumps when I think about that…it was just palpable…and it was manifested here as John Trudell said, "The water tells us we are one." I think Eureka Springs kind of embodies the spirit of that, and that this experience brought us that.*[113]

Chapter 17

THE NEW DOWNSTREAM PEOPLE

O ne person who never gave up believing that Eureka Springs could be a model city for clean water was Barbara Harmony (formerly Hovland). When the revised wastewater treatment plan was released in 1978, she used her position as classical music disc jockey for the local radio station, broadcasting from the top of the Crescent Hotel, to inform her fellow citizens. She read the entire report on the air while playing Wagner. During the exfiltration study, she had been one of the coordinators for the Citizen Advisory Committee. When her son Ben came home to Oak Hill from his first day of public school and ran directly to the outhouse in the backyard, she asked him about it. He told her that he couldn't "go in the water." It gave her hope that she was perhaps making progress.

Many believed that its history as a place of healing made Eureka Springs special; however, the philosophy of water stewardship was hard to sell. The movement got a boost in 1993, when the EPA announced that it would start organizing, using the watershed as its basic unit.

The 1980s had seen a boom in tourism in the whole region. By the mid-'90s, another issue was raising its ugly head: would the town be a side trip from the "Country Music Capital," Branson, Missouri, forty-five miles to the north, or maintain its own identity as a historic spa town? The 1994 city elections were so contentious that many voters protested by voting for a candidate who had recently died. She won by one vote.

New ideas were sought during the next year. Consultants August St. John (marketing), Patricia Michael (permaculture) and James Graebner (transportation) were among those who encouraged sanity. In Graebner's report to the city council on January 16, 1996, he said "Downtown is the Jewel" and that even Disney could not make a Historic District. New traffic controls limited tour buses and large delivery trucks to certain times and areas, which helped to protect the ambiance and the aging infrastructure of the Historic District.

New Springs Projects

The turn of the twenty-first century brought renewed efforts to clean up the springs. In 2000, the One Clean Spring Project began. Barbara Harmony, National Water Center coordinator; Susan Lourne, former Parks and Recreation director; and Kirby Murray, former Public Works director, held a series of meetings to determine if a spring could be made potable.

Research into the feasibility of eliminating pollutants from a spring in order to develop a drinking water source began with Public Works Department staff testing springs for fecal coliform on a regular basis from January 2001 to October 2002. Basin and Magnetic were identified as possible sites. The project hit a snag when they met with Mike Mathis, a consulting engineer, who told them that according to federal regulations stipulated in the Clean Water Act, a public drinking water source needs to be 350 feet away from a sewer line and some type of purification system is necessary.

In 2002, the Basin Spring Committee prepared a plan. Members of the committee included Butch Berry, Rick Armalini, Johnice Cross and James DeVito. They were looking into providing spring water to the public at Basin Park. They worked with Pressley Engineering to design a plan for filtration and disinfection. However, they, too, ran into Arkansas Health Department regulations. The proposal included a description and pictures of the spring as it exists in the tunnels under the Improvements of 1890, at which time the cement semicircle, limestone walls, wishing well and fountain were constructed. Even the original pipe work and area under the band shell, added at a later date, were illustrated in the report.

Watershed Education

Barbara Harmony and Kate Cooper directed a daylong workshop about the springs, called "Our Springs: A Watershed Education Program," in February 2003, and a series of public service announcements followed. Judi Selle wrote the proposal funded by the Environmental Protection Agency (EPA) and managed by the local Community Development Partnership (CDP).

A family enjoys Grotto Spring Park, autumn 2004. *Photo by Richard Quick.*

Guest speakers came from Fayetteville, Little Rock and Austin, Texas. Dr. Van Brahana spoke of the geologic and hydrologic features of the area. Ellen McNulty told about watershed management, and Patricia Michael described landscaping to improve spring water flow and quality. During lunch, Kerby Murry presented the efforts of the Eureka Springs Public Works Department to monitor spring water and fix broken sewer lines. Public Works also handled the advanced registration process. Eighth graders from Eureka Springs Middle School came to listen to Van Brahana's speech.

That afternoon, Patricia Michael took people from the Crescent Hotel down to Grotto Spring to learn about the recharge zone. She discovered a sink hole above the grotto. Marty and Elise Roenigk, owners of the Crescent Hotel, sponsored a project to learn about Grotto Spring and to do ongoing maintenance of the recharge area.

SPRINGS COMMITTEE

The Springs Committee, formed by the Parks and Recreation Commission in 2004, has been chaired by Barbara Harmony, who presented the original proposal. At that time, the main short-range goals were to form a Springs Committee to develop public awareness of the springs and to place the One Clean Spring project among the commission's top priorities. Long-range goals included managing storm runoff in city-owned green zones and partnering with residents and businesses near the springs and in recharge areas.

Committee members, all local residents, shared their expertise in a series of presentations in March and April 2007. Jim Helwig, a PhD geologist, spoke about the geology of the springs. Andrea Radwell, a stream ecologist with a doctorate in the field, discussed the importance of biodiversity in assessing environmental quality of streams and springs. Shawna Miller, coordinator of the Kings River Watershed Partnership, led a hands-on demonstration on Leatherwood Creek. Jamie Froelich talked about her research in microbiology and the kinds of microbes found in the springs and watershed.

Another Springs Committee project was to put medallions on storm drains around town that read, "Drains to Springs Eureka Springs" and have a picture of a crayfish on them. The Williams crayfish is a species common in the springs and Leatherwood Creek watershed but rare elsewhere. In that same year, 2008, the committee produced a four-color brochure, *Living in the Leatherwood Creek Watershed: A Citizen's Guide*, to inform citizens about the dos and don'ts of living on karst. "Karst terrain forms when slightly acidic rain and surface water dissolves rock, usually limestone."

The committee made a "State of the Springs" report in 2010 after working with U.S. Geological Survey scientists to monitor spring water. Among their conclusions was the statement that it is possible to clean the springs.

FREE THE SPRING

Basin Spring was the starting point of the original town site survey in 1879. Basin Park has been and continues to serve as an outdoor civic center. Events of many kinds, from grand opera to watermelon-eating contests, occur with frequency throughout each year.

The Improvements of 1890 created a walking surface raised thirteen feet above the spring basin. After a decade, the site had become well worn by thousands of health seekers who walked about day after day to get water from the spring. Sanitation had become an issue, and with the improvements, the basin was hidden below and the water piped to faucets above.

A new campaign has been launched to create a presentation well, similar to the stonework circle at Sweet Spring, to allow people to see the basin again. At a public meeting on December 6, 2011, parks commissioner Stephen Foster showed historic photos, as well as pictures of parts of the park badly in need of repairs. Bill Featherstone, Parks Commission chairman, said, "This park is getting toward the end of its current life and we want to prepare the park for the next 100 years." The projected cost of $300,000 for construction will be paid from donations, not public funds.[114]

Basin Spring is, and has been from the beginning, the heart of the city.

Conclusion

RECHARGE!

When visitors come into the Eureka Springs Historical Museum in the historic Calef House on South Main Street, one of their first questions is, "What can you tell us about the springs?" This is usually followed by: Where are they located? How many are there? Can we see the water? Do they really heal? The springs have touched so many lives.

For residents, the relationship to the springs is somewhat complex. They are our namesake and our responsibility. Among the people are descendants of pioneer families, while many are more recent transplants. Some still have a raw nerve when they recall the citywide action of thirty years ago. One town patriarch recalled that the centennial was the last time the people all pulled together, since everyone could get behind the restoration efforts. Others believe that those efforts didn't go far enough. Some cringe at any talk of springs because they fear cleanup would mean additional burdens on this service-oriented populace.

The fact is that the springs continue to make news. In the last year, record rainfalls caused a collapse of a hillside near Grotto Spring. The Free Basin Spring proposal has found a home in the Parks Department. New hiking trails have been constructed near Oil and Johnson Springs. The springs were featured on Chuck Dovach's *Explore Arkansas* on the Arkansas Educational Television Network. The Springs Committee continues a monitoring program and informs the public in a variety of ways, including "Springs Talk," a monthly column in the *Lovely County Citizen*. The Eureka Springs Chamber of Commerce continues to proclaim the natural beauty of the environment as an attraction to the area.

In concluding this book about the City of Healing Waters, we would like to give our answers to some frequently asked questions.

WHERE ARE THE SPRINGS?

All around you. Since we now know that the springs are recharged from the hillsides around them, not from distant or deep sources, any rain falling on the ridge tops or hillsides of Eureka Springs is likely to be discharged in one or more of the springs.

The five major valleys where springs flow from the ground can be thought of as a hand if you are standing near the train depot beside Leatherwood Creek facing south toward the city. Imagine the thumb is Dairy Hollow. The little finger points to Magnetic and Mystic Springs in Magnetic Hollow. The ring finger indicates Mill Hollow, where Minnehaha and Ozarka Springs flow. The middle finger is Water Street, where the loop of Steele and Douglas Streets are the location of several springs such as Cave, Little Eureka and Carry Nation, among others. Finally, the index finger is Main Street, where Conway and Calef Springs are found. Spring Street from Basin to Grotto follows the contour of the hill between the "pointer" and the thumb.

Other springs are located in the valleys on the opposite side of West Mountain in the Black Bass Lake and Lake Leatherwood areas. All the lakes, including Lake Lucerne, are spring-fed reservoirs.

Thinking in terms of the entire groundwater system and not just where the springs discharge is an important and challenging idea to grasp. In between the fingers in our model, the ledges and ridge tops are at higher elevations. All of these ridges are the recharge zone for the springs of Eureka Springs.

The Chattanooga shale layer, being impermeable, determines the location of many springs about halfway up the hillside. Others, such as Magnetic and Gadd, discharge from the lower groundwater system.

Blue Spring, a few miles west of town, is the exception to the rule, as its source may be from very deep and a good deal farther from its discharge point.

HOW MANY SPRINGS ARE THERE?

Pick a number. Sources differ in their counts of the springs. Johnston's 1884 guide gave the number as 42. In the 1950s, the favored number was 63. The exfiltration study in 1980 included 110 sites and mapped recharge areas of 76 springs. In that study, Tom Aley explained that there are so many because they are small, compared to some Ozark springs that drain very large areas. Secondly, the two-layer groundwater system contributes to creating more springs.

WHERE CAN I SEE SPRING WATER?

The best places to see spring water are more than a dozen spring parks that are cared for by the Eureka Springs Parks and Recreation Commission. A brochure with a map is available. A number of gardeners have taken up the care of the grounds around the springs through the past three decades. In

Harding Spring, 2008. *Photo by Barbara Scott.*

recent years, gardening has been the artistic creation and devoted nurturing of Don E. Allen. Visitors are encouraged to respect the privacy of those living near the springs outside the city-owned reservations.

DO THE SPRINGS REALLY HEAL?

They certainly had that reputation with thousands of testimonials of those who benefited. Only a few hundred names and stories have survived to this day of those who were healed. In the skepticism of the twenty-first-century mindset, it would be easy to write off these stories as hype. We believe that sells short the challenges faced by those early pioneers.

There are also questions about whether the Indians used the springs for healing. The legend that Native Americans left their weapons outside the area where the springs are located because it was sacred to them has been scoffed at by some archaeologists and historians as being the romantic creation of the European descendants who appropriated the use of the springs for their own entrepreneurial ventures.

Around 1900, Dr. C.F. Ellis, one of Eureka Springs' early medical men, was moved to figurative speech when he described nature's role as an aid in healing:

> *Here blow the cooling winds, and zephyrs soft as maiden's kiss of love, or mother's fond caress to her first born; and yearning skies of deepest blue lean down as if to bless so fair a scene. Here sun's warm splendor and the soft and tender light of moon and watching stars shine fairer than on other lands. And without sound of words, but in these loveliest scenes, that all might understand, no matter what their speech, God wrote a poem:*

> *Here nature paused, and then she wrought*
> *On canvas vast, a wondrous thought.*
> *She piled the hills to mountain height—*
> *They rose majestic in their might,*
> *And smiled from their far-reaching crest*
> *On vales below, in beauty dressed;*
> *And in her sparkling waters pure*
> *She placed her magic power to cure,*
> *Then with a touch of perfect clime*
> *She left the praise to man, and time.*

Crescent Dragonwagon, noted author and founder of the Dairy Hollow Writers' Colony, had this to say in 1997:

If the town no longer cures physical diseases (including, according to the accounts, everything from scrofula and malaria to, as the Victorians delicately put it, "gentleman's inability"), it relieves other modern afflictions. Fear of crime, alienation, and disorientation in a too big, too fast world, the anxiety that sets in when everything, from motels to airports to fast-food restaurants, looks like everything else, everywhere: these uneasinesses are what Eureka cures now, still.

Eureka looks, tastes, and smells different because it is. The streets still double back on themselves; the view from the East Mountain overlook still astonishes; the woods are still crosshatched with walking paths. I always suggest visitors get a massage, eat a really good meal of slow food at any of a dozen or so chef-owned restaurants, buy something made and sold only right here, nap, relax.

I think mostly we Eurekans realize we're all healing from something, and that on this brief, mysterious, lush sojourn through our lives, we are all tourists. Eureka's got a long tradition of helpfulness in this regard.

Eureka Springs was founded in a sudden rush, with restoration of health as its central focus. While mining, farming, timber and railroads were minor players, healing water was the star.

NOTES

Chapter 1

1. Biggs et al., *Glencoe Biology*.
2. Aley, *Exfiltration Study*.
3. Miller et al., *Continents in Collision*.
4. Ficher, "Geologic Evolution."
5. Radwell, *Biodiversity in the Ozarks*.

Chapter 2

6. Waters, *Book of the Hopi*, 41.
7. Bailey, *Osage and the Invisible World*, 63; Mathews, *The Osages*, 10.
8. Zedeña and Laluk, *Cultural Affiliation*, 20.
9. Sabo, "Native American Prehistory," in Whayne et al., *Arkansas*, 5.
10. Schambach, "Tom's Brook Culture." 8.
11. "Blue Spring Shelter."
12. Schambach, "Tom's Brook Culture," 8.
13. Gibson, "Poverty Point."
14. Zedeña and Laluk, *Cultural Affiliation*.
15. Goss, "Breckenridge Flute."
16. Pauketat, *Cahokia*, 1–2.
17. Rollings, "Living in a Graveyard," in Whayne, *Cultural Encounters*, 38.

CHAPTER 3

18. Rollings, "Living in a Graveyard," in Whayne, *Cultural Encounters*, 44.
19. Sabo, *Paths of Our Children*, 46–47.
20. Mathews, *The Osages*.
21. Ibid., 81
22. Ibid., 154–56
23. Ibid., 177–78 143–45, 695.
24. Whayne, *Cultural Encounters*, 122–23.
25. Newman, *Black Dog Trail*, 18–19.
26. Whayne, *Cultural Encounters*, 122.
27. Brown, *American Spa*, 11.

CHAPTER 4

28. Garrett, interview.
29. Westphal, "John and Lucy Harp."
30. Lewis, *History of Jasper County*, 153.
31. Haden, "Huntsville."
32. Zedeña and Laluk, *Cultural Affiliation*.

CHAPTER 5

33. Gentry, "Rock Springs Church," 458.
34. Huddleston, Rose and Wood, *Steamboats and Ferries*, 12.
35. Tibbs, *Joy to the Afflicted*.
36. *Goodspeed History*, 371.
37. Ingenthron, "Civil War Atrocities."
38. *Goodspeed History*, 371–72.
39. Clark, *Letters and Diaries*, 37–38.
40. Trelease, *White Terror*, 154.

CHAPTER 6

41. Tibbs, *Joy to the Afflicted*.
42. Pinkley-Call, "Stories," 303.
43. Goodspeed History, 372.

CHAPTER 7

44. Valenčius, *Health of the Country*, 153.
45. Westphal, *Eureka Chronicles*, 23.
46. Dew, "From Trails to Rails," 206.
47. Pinkley-Call, *Pioneer Tales*, 45.
48. Bailey, "Matlock Legend."
49. Westphal, *Eureka Chronicles*, 28.
50. Miller, "Then and Now," 1–2.
51. Kalklosch, *Healing Fountain*, 48.
52. Clark, *Letters and Diaries*, 232.
53. Dew, "From Trails to Rails," 206.
54. *Time-Echo*, March 1880.

CHAPTER 8

55. Westphal, *Eureka Chronicles*, 19–20.
56. Kalklosch, *Healing Fountain*, 21.
57. Pinkley-Call, *Pioneer Tales*, 59–60.
58. Hartman, "Amon Jesse Fortner."
59. Miller, "An Old Eureka Paper," 7.
60. Cutter, *Cutter's Guide*, 34.
61. Westphal, *A Fame Not Easily Forgotten.*
62. *Daily Graphic*, 1882.

CHAPTER 9

63. Dew, "From Trails to Rails."
64. *Daily Graphic*, 1882.
65. Goodspeed History, 381.
66. Sell, "Eureka's Springs."
67. Johnston, *The Eureka Springs.*
68. Hitchcock and Martin, News Bulletin; Kalklosch, *Healing Fountain*, 34.
69. "History of the Crescent Hotel."
70. Sell, "Eureka's Springs."
71. *Eureka Springs, Arkansas*, 21.
72. Johnston, *The Eureka Springs*, 12.

73. Reese, *Medical Journal.*
74. Kappen, "Bath Houses of Eureka Springs."

CHAPTER 10

75. *Six Scenic Walking Tours.*
76. Johnston, *The Eureka Springs.*
77. *Six Scenic Walking Tours.*

CHAPTER 11

78. Reese, *Medical Journal.*
79. Moyers, "From Quackery to Qualification."
80. Miller, "Dr. Reed's Plan," 19.
81. Miller, advertisement in *Points* (January–March 1900); Miller, "Eureka Water Co.," February 1901.
82. Thompson, "Address."
83. Johnston, *The Eureka Springs.*
84. Kappen, "Bath Houses of Eureka Springs."
85. *Daily Times-Echo,* "Radio-Activity."
86. "Eureka Water and Cancer."
87. *Drink to Your Health.*

CHAPTER 12

88. Fischbeck and Farrow, *Improving Regulation.*
89. Sell, "Eureka's Springs."
90. Ibid.

CHAPTER 13

91. Pinkley-Call *A Stair-Step Town,* 25–26.
92. Pinkley-Call, Papers; Moore, Letter to Phil Bullock.
93. Pinkley-Call, Papers.
94. Howerton, "Glen Ward Dresbach."

95. Monroe, *Poetry.*
96. Rayburn, "Eureka Springs."
97. Sell, "Eureka's Springs."
98. Aley, *Exfiltration Study.*

CHAPTER 14

99. Martin, *Gathering Days.*
100. Ibid.
101. Simpson, "Earnest Otto Rayburn."

CHAPTER 15

102. Robertson, *Peaceful Storm.*
103. Martin, *Gathering Days.*
104. Ibid.
105. Ibid.

CHAPTER 16

106. Bradt, *We All Live Downstream.*
107. Martin, *Gathering Days.*
108. Summary, 1984.
109. Ibid.
110. Martin, *Gathering Days.*
111. Aley, *Exfiltration Study.*
112. Ibid.
113. Martin, *Gathering Days.*

CHAPTER 17

114. Boyette, "Basin Park Project."

BIBLIOGRAPHY

Aley, Thomas. *Exfiltration Study of Eureka Springs*. Protem, MO: Ozark Underground Laboratory, 1981.

Arkansas Preservation Society. "Blue Spring Shelter, Carroll County." www.arkansaspreservation.com/historic-properties/_search_nomination_popup.asp?id=330.

Bailey, Gerrick A., ed. *The Osage and the Invisible World: From the Works of Francis La Flesche*. Norman: University of Oklahoma Press, 1995.

Bailey, Winnie S. "The Matlock Legend." The Compiled Research of Winnie S. Bailey on the Matlock Family Ancestry, 2000. http://homepages.rootsweb.ancestry.com/~szmatlok/Bailey/2-7.html.

Biggs, Alton, et al. *Glencoe Biology*. New York: McGraw-Hill Companies, Inc., 2007.

Blair, M.Z. *Preliminary Informal Report on Investigation of Ultra-Violet Ray Treatment of Water from Public Springs at Eureka Springs*. State Board of Health, September 1921.

————. *Report on an Investigation of the Prevalence of Typhoid Fever at Eureka Springs, to State Health Officer C.W. Garrison*. December 20, 1920.

Boyette, Nicky. "Basin Park Project Gets Public Input." *Lovely County Citizen* 13, no. 3 (December 8, 2011): 7, 27.

Bradt, Terri, prod. *We All Live Downstream: Songs for Living Water*. The Water Center Eureka Springs audio cassette, 1884. CD, 2009.

Brown, Dee. *The American Spa*. Little Rock, AR: Rose Publishing Company, 1982.

Burns, Louis. *A History of the Osage People*. N.p., 1989. Reprint, Tuscaloosa: University of Alabama Press, 2004.

Clark, Wayne, ed. *The Letters and Diaries of Isaac A. Clarke: Innovative Educator in Post Civil War Arkansas*. Victoria, BC: Trafford Publishing, 2006.

Costner, Pat, Holly Gettings and Glenna Booth. *We All Live Downstream: A Guide to Waste Treatment That Stops Water Pollution.* Eureka Springs, AR: Waterworks Publishing Company, 1986.

Cutter, Charles. *Cutter's Guide to the Eureka Springs of Arkansas.* St. Louis, MO: Cutter and Trump, 1884.

Daily Graphic [New York]. "Eureka Springs, Ark.—A City Built in Less than Three Years—Its Wonderful Waters." May 9, 1882.

Daily Times-Echo. "Radio-Activity in Eureka Springs Water." Arkansas travelers' edition, June 1907.

Dellinger, Samuel. "Folklore Festival Program." Manuscript collection 204, Box 19 # 14. Special Collections, University of Arkansas–Fayetteville, 1934.

Dew, Lew A. "From Trails to Rails in Eureka Springs." *Arkansas Historical Quarterly* 41, no. 3 (Autumn 1982): 203–14.

Dragonwagon, Crescent. "Eureka Springs Home, Apparently." In *Somewhere Apart: "My Favorite Place in Arkansas," Arkansas Residents Past and Present.* Compiled by the staff of the *Arkansas Times* and University of Arkansas Press. Fayetteville: University of Arkansas Press, 1997. 19–25.

Drink from the Fountain of Youth. Commercial Club booklet, n.d.

Drink to Your Health and Get It at Eureka Springs. Commercial Club booklet, 1926.

Ellis, C.F., MD. "Power of Water." *Daily Times-Echo,* April 24, 1905. Reprint of address delivered to the Railway Passenger Agents' Association, 1902.

Eureka Springs, Arkansas. St. Louis, MO: Woodward and Tiernan Printing Co., 1887. Eureka Springs Historical Museum Collection D-B44.

"Eureka Water and Cancer." Flashlight 1917 Microfilm Carroll County Historical and Genealogical Society Berryville, Arkansas.

Ficher, Lynn S. "The Geologic Evolution of Virginia and the Mid-Atlantic Region." Department of Geology and Environmental Studies, James Madison University.

Fischbeck, Paul Stelling, and R. Scott Farrow. *Improving Regulation: Cases in Environment, Health, and Safety.* Resources for the Future, 2001.

Garrett, Kreglyn. Interview with the authors, November 11, 2010.

Gentry, Alice Baker. "Rock Springs Church, Carroll County, Arkansas." *Arkansas Historical Quarterly* 6, no. 4 (Winter 1947): 458–61.

Gibson, Jon L. "Poverty Point." University of Southwestern Louisiana, 1996. www.crt.state.la.us/archaeology/virtualbooks/poverpoi/popo.htm.

Goodspeed History of Carroll County, Arkansas. Berryville, AR: Braswell Printing, n.d. Reprint of *Northwest Arkansas History.* N.p.: Goodspeed Publishing Company, 1889.

Goss, Clint. "The Breckenridge Flute." *Flutopedia: An Encyclopedia for the Native American Flute,* January 12, 2012. www.flutopedia.com/breckenridge.htm.

Haden, Rebecca, and Joy Russell. "Huntsville (Madison County)." *Encyclopedia of Arkansas*, 2011. http://encyclopediaofarkansas.net/encyclopedia/entry-detail.aspx?search=1&entryID=930.

Hammersley, Florence. "In Nature's Beautiful Realm." *Daily Times-Echo*, 1905. First stanza also found in a scrapbook at the Eureka Springs Historical Museum.

Hartman, Viola. "Amon Jesse Fortner." *White River Valley Historical Quarterly* 7, no. 11 (Spring 1982).

Hinkle, Jim. "Wm. R. Jackson, b. 1769–1773, Cane Creek, Orange, NC." Ancestry.com.

"History of the Crescent Hotel." Crescent Hotel, 2007. www.crescent-hotel.com/history.htm.

Hitchcock and Martin. News Bulletin, November 1881. Microfilm. Carroll County Historical and Genealogical Society.

Howerton, Phillip. "Glenn Ward Dresbach (1889–1968)." *Encyclopedia of Arkansas History and Culture*. http://encyclopediaofarkansas.net/encyclopedia/entry-detail.aspx?entryID=3074.

Huddleston, Duane, Sammie Cantrell Rose and Pat Taylor Wood. *Steamboats and Ferries on the White River: A Heritage Revisited*. Fayetteville: University of Arkansas Press, 1998.

Huntsville, Arkansas city website. http://www.huntsvillear.org.

Ingenthron, Elmo. "Civil War Atrocities in the Upper White River Valley." *White River Valley Historical Quarterly* 1, no. 4. (Fall 1962).

Johnston, W.W., MD. *The Eureka Springs, Arkansas*. St. Louis, MO: A. Ungar & Co., 1884.

Kalklosch, L.J. The *Healing Fountain*. St. Louis, MO: Chambers' Print, 1881.

Kappen, Charles V. "Bath Houses of Eureka Springs." *Carroll County Historical Quarterly* 23, no. 1 (Spring 1983).

Kay, Marvin. "Goforth-Saindon and Huntsville Mounds." In *Archaeology of Prehistoric Native Americans: An Encyclopedia*. Guy E. Gibbon and Kenneth M. Ames. 1998. http://books.google.com/books?id=_0u2y_SVnmoC&q=Goforth#v=snippet&q=Goforth&f=false.

Kearney, John W. *Eureka Springs: The Resort of the Ozarks*. N.p., 1907. Special Collections, University of Arkansas–Fayetteville.

Lewis, Renessa. "1883 History of Jasper County, Missouri." http://freepages.genealogy.rootsweb.ancestry.com/~rslewis/bios/1883/1.htm.

Martin, Sandy. *Gathering Days*. Eureka Springs Historical Museum interviews. Video. Procomm, 2009.

Mathews, John Joseph. *The Osages: Children of the Middle Waters*. Norman: University of Oklahoma Press, 1961.

Miller, Giles, ed. "An Old Eureka Paper." *Points* 1, no. 1 (January–March 1900): 7.

———. "Dr. Reed's Plan." *Points* 1, no. 1 (January–March 1900): 19.

———. "Eureka Water Co." *Points* 2, no. 2 (February 1901): advertisement.

———. "Then and Now." *Points* 1, no. 1 (January–March 1900): 1–2.

Miller, Russell, et al. *Continents in Collision: Planet Earth Series*. Alexandria, VA: Time-Life Books, 1983.

Mills, Nellie Alice. *Early Days at Eureka Springs, 1880–1892*. Monett, MO: Free Will Baptist Gem, 1949.

———. *Other Days at Eureka Springs*. Monett, MO: Free Will Baptist Gem, 1950.

———. *A Story of the Ozarks*. Eureka Springs Historical Museum D-M8.

Monroe, Harriet, ed. *Poetry* 33, no. 1 (October 1928).

Moore, Gerry. Letter to Phil Bullock, November 17, 1978. Springs File, Eureka Springs Historical Museum.

Moyers, David M. "From Quackery to Qualification: Arkansas Medical and Drug Legislation, 1881–1909." *Arkansas Historical Quarterly* 35, no. 1 (Spring 1976): 3–26.

Newman, Tillie Karns. *The Black Dog Trail: The Story of the Osage Indians*. Boston, MA: Christopher Publishing House, 1957.

Pauketat, Timothy R. *Cahokia: Ancient America's Great City on the Mississippi*. New York: Viking, 2009.

Pinkley-Call, Cora. Papers 1930–1966. Special Collections University of Arkansas–Fayetteville.

———. *Pioneer Tales*. N.p., 1930. http://persi.heritagequestonline.com/hqoweb/library/do/books/results/image?urn=urn:proquest:US;glhbooks;Genealogy-glh36348616;54;-1.

———. *Stair-Step-Town*. Little Rock, AR: Jenkins Enterprises North, 1952.

———. "Stories about the Origin of Eureka Springs." *Arkansas Historical Quarterly* 5, no. 3 (Autumn 1946): 297–307.

Radwell, Andrea J., PhD. *Biodiversity of the Ozarks*. Presentation at Clear Springs High School, May 4, 2007. Video.

Rayburn, Earnest Otto. "Eureka Springs, Experiencing No Shortage of Water." Article in scrapbook. Special Collections, University of Arkansas–Fayetteville.

———. *Forty Years in The Ozarks: An Autobiography Ozark Guide Press*. Eureka Springs, AR, 1957.

Reese, W.A., ed. *Medical Journal*. Eureka Springs, 1893. Microfilm. Mullins Library, University of Arkansas–Fayetteville.

Robertson, Charles F. *The Peaceful Storm*. Green Forest, AR: New Leaf Press, 1985.

Sabo, George, III. *Paths of Our Children: The Historic Indians of Arkansas.* Arkansas Archaeology Society, 2001.

Schambach, Frank. "Tom's Brook Culture." *Encyclopedia of Arkansas*, July 23, 2008. http://encyclopediaofarkansas.net/encyclopedia/entry-detail.aspx?entryID=546.

Schambach, Frank, and Leslie Newell. *Crossroads of the Past: 12,000 Years of Indian Life in Arkansas*. Fayetteville: Arkansas Archaeological Survey, 1990.

Sell, Mary Jean. "Eureka's Springs." Transcribed from city's permanent ordinance books by clerk-treasurer, 2007–8.

Simpson, Ethel C. "Earnest Otto Rayburn, An Early Promoter of the Ozarks." *Arkansas Historical Quarterly* 58, no. 2 (Summer 1999): 160–79.

Six Scenic Walking Tours in Historic Eureka Springs Arkansas. Pamphlet. Eureka Springs Preservation Society, 1997.

Summary of Public Participation Program Eureka Springs, Arkansas C-050378-02. Fayetteville, AR: McClelland Consulting Engineers, Inc., April 23, 1984.

Thompson, Richard R. "Address Delivered to Texas Bottled Water Dealers Convention at Texas A. & M. College, March 5, 1956, by Richard R. Thompson, Shipper of Ozarka Water from Eureka Springs and Hot Springs, Arkansas." Rayburn Scrapbook.

Tibbs, John S. *Joy to the Afflicted*. Pamphlet. Eureka Springs Historical Museum (D-T1), 1881.

Trelease, Allen W. *White Terror: The Ku Klux Klan Conspiracy and Southern Reconstruction*. New York: Harper and Row, 1971.

Tyler, Virginia. "Hiking Club Highlights." *Eureka Springs Times-Echo*, 1968–1969. Special Collections, University of Arkansas–Fayetteville.

Underwood, Paula. *The Walking People: A Native American Oral History*. San Anselmo, CA: Tribe of Two Press, 1993.

Valenčius, Conevery Bolton. *The Health of the Country: How American Settlers Understood Themselves and Their Land*. New York: Basic Books, 2002.

Waring, George E., Jr. "Draining of a Village." *Harper's New Monthly Magazine* 59, no. 349 (June 1879). Cornell University Library. http://www.sewerhistory.org/articles/design/1879_ah03/article.pdf.

———. *Removal of Destructive Organic Wastes*. Baltimore, MD: Guggenheimer, Weil and Co., 1886. http://books.google.com/books?id=pv5aAAAAQAAJ&pg=PA7&dq=George+Waring+Destructive+Organic+Waste&hl=en&sa=X&ei=1MJDT7TyGsSziQLMwLnTAQ&ved=0CDsQ6AEwAA#v=onepage&q=George%20Waring%20Destructive%20Organic%20Waste&f=false.

Waters, Frank. *The Book of the Hopi*. New York: Ballantine Books, 1963.

Westphal, June. *The Eureka Chronicles: Ten Decades of History of Eureka Springs—from 1990s to 1980s*. Eureka Springs, AR: Penguin Graphics, 1987.

———. "John and Lucy (Vaughan) Harp" and other unpublished family genealogical research, 2011.

Westphal, June, and Osterhage, Catherine. *A Fame Not Easily Forgotten: An Autobiography of Eureka Springs*. N.p., 1970. 2nd ed., 2010.

Whayne, Jeannie, ed. *Cultural Encounters in the Early South: Indians and Europeans in Arkansas*. Fayetteville: University of Arkansas Press, 1995.

Whayne, Jeannie, et al. *Arkansas: A Narrative History*. Fayetteville: University of Arkansas Press, 2002.

Zedeña, María Nieves, and Nicholas Laluk. *Cultural Affiliation Statement Buffalo National River, Arkansas*. Tucson: University of Arizona, 2008.